what
NOT
to name your baby

Also by
JOE BORGENICHT

The Baby Owner's Manual (with Louis Borgenicht)
The Action Hero's Handbook (with David Borgenicht)
The Action Heroine's Handbook (with Jennifer Worick)
Doggy Days (with Melanie Borgenicht)
The Reality TV Handbook (with John Saade)
Undercover Golf (with Richard Robinson)

what NOT to name your baby

by Joe Borgenicht

SIMON SPOTLIGHT ENTERTAINMENT
New York   London   Toronto   Sydney

SIMON SPOTLIGHT ENTERTAINMENT
An imprint of Simon & Schuster
1230 Avenue of the Americas, New York, New York 10020
Text copyright © 2005 by True West Productions, Inc.
SIMON SPOTLIGHT ENTERTAINMENT and related logo are
trademarks of Simon & Schuster, Inc.
Manufactured in the U.S.A.
First Edition 10 9 8 7 6 5 4 3 2 1
Library of Congress Cataloging-in-Publication Data
Borgenicht, Joe.
What not to name your baby / by Joe Borgenicht.—1st ed.
p. cm.
ISBN 0-689-87581-9
1. Names, Personal—Humor. I. Title.
PN6231.N24B67 2005 818'.602—dc22   2004023926

acknowledgments

Thanks first and foremost to my crack team of corporate researchers: Evan Labb, Laura Kvinge, Ryan Lufkin, and Ms. Ceri Jones. Without you there would be no book—and without the book, you would have had a lot more time to kill. Thanks also to Tucker Fudpucker for writing the foreword and sharing the pain of his childhood and current life with our readers (my apologies to the U.K. Tucker Fudpucker whom I prank called when visiting the country back in '83). Endless thanks to Ryan Harbage and Jen Bergstrom for making this book a reality. And finally, thanks to my wife, "Baby Love," son, "Bugs," and dog, "Satie-Face," for not disowning me for my inability to invent armor-clad nicknames for all three of them.

table of contents

A Fudpucker by any other name . . .

It's bad enough that my dad's side of the family had to endure a surname like ours. But when he and mom decided to try to cancel out the pain of being born a Fudpucker by naming me Tucker, they were horribly misguided.

When it comes to naming . . . no wrongs make a right.

Take it from me. The wrong name will doom your child for life. I started out all right until my mother stopped home-schooling me in the fourth grade. She said, "Tucker Fudpucker, it's time for you to face the world." Until that time I had no idea there was anything wrong with my name. In fact, due to my somewhat sheltered childhood, I entered the fourth grade thinking that everyone was a Fudpucker (we had lots of cousins who also had to eat their daily dose of "Prozac" candy).

When I was thirteen, I graduated from the sixth grade. It wasn't because my mother's homeschooling wasn't sufficient. (In fact, Mom had me on the fast track for Harvard). Rather, my education came to a standstill when I entered public school. I was caught in a daily quagmire. I would return home from school—in tears—and explain to my mother that some of the kids at school had rearranged the first letters of my first and last names. Every time I said the F-word to explain what they said, I got my mouth rinsed with soap.

My bar mitzvah wasn't any better. When the cantor sang my call to read the Torah (my name in Hebrew is pronounced "TZUH-ker PHUD-puh-kher") the entire synagogue burst into laughter and didn't stop until all of the schnapps and herring were gone. You'd think I'd have developed a thicker skin. But it never goes away.

I'm just as guilty as anybody. When I went away to college I unofficially changed my name to Joe. There were fewer jokes, but I found myself making up for all of the fun that was made of me by judging other people's names. Once I went on a blind date with a woman named Xochilt (pronounced "SO-chee"). When I asked her what her name meant, she said, "It's Aztec, for flower." "Oh," I said. "Well, my name's Joe. It's American, for coffee."

All my life I suppose I've been sabotaging relationships like that. There's only been one woman who stuck by me after she learned that her possible married name could be Fudpucker. And that was sweet Chastity . . . the one that got away. She would have accepted the name Chastity Fudpucker. In her line of work as a professional dancer, her real last name didn't matter much. We would have gone all the way, too, if it hadn't been for her friends Star, Octavia, and Pleasure. One night Chastity and I were in a special room—so special in fact, the owners had named it "The Champagne Room"—and Star, Octavia, and Pleasure found out what my last name was. They stopped dancing and started in, just like everybody else. Chastity tried to stick up for me, but the peer pressure was too much. (Plus, whenever I ran out of cash, she always got a little moody for some reason.) I never saw her again.

I guess you could say I've found my niche, now. The asbestos factory is a pretty good place to work since none of the other employees speak English. Oh, don't get me wrong, occasionally I overhear a couple of them snickering a "Fudpucker" or two. But they never say anything to my face.

If I had any advice, it would be this: Stick with the standards, spell it like it is, and at all costs avoid rhyming.

Sincerely,
Tucker Fudpucker

introduction

One of the greatest challenges new parents will face (pre-baby) is finding the right name, with the right rhythm, that the fewest number of school children could potentially make fun of. To aid in this challenge there are numerous books and Web sites available that can help you name your child by offering meaning, metaphor, genealogy, religion, race, and pop icon background, among other things.

But now, there is a new essential standard in baby naming: what *not* to name your baby! Think about it (particularly if you have a couple of the 35,000 name books). How are you going to sift through all of that? Granted, you've got a nine-month lead time, but still . . . Even if you start your search at conception, it's an average of 130 names a day. Who's got time? (If you do, please forgive us. . . . It's just the first of many offensive comments you'll come across when you read on. And by the way, no more apologizing. This is it. Everybody is a target. From Dakota to Cheyenne. The names, that is, not the cities. The cities are fine.)

The approach is simple. This book will tell you exactly how *not* to name your baby. That's at least half the battle!

For some reason many new parents subscribe to the belief that a name dictates the possibilities for the rest of a new baby's life. Nowhere is that more true than when you name your baby wrong. Take, for example, Einstein. Good name. Lots of potential. But chances are, by the time your son (or, if you're one of those *really* clever parents, daughter) navigates elementary school with comments like, "Nice shot, Einstein," or "Who knows the answer? Einstein?" he'll wind up with such a complex that you'll be lucky if he makes it through basic algebra after five years of college.

In this book you will find new rules for how *not* to name your children. Then you'll find a slew of names that you absolutely positively cannot use, complete with a pronunciations, definitions, reasons you cannot use them, and, on a more positive note, a limited number of loopholes just in case the wrong name is really right. And finally, to make your journey bearable, you'll find trivia-filled sidebars with information like: famous plumbers, how many Jennys there are in America, and the most unpopular names of 2000.

The reality is that your children will probably change their names on their own when they can't take it anymore. Or at least when they land a film career. As a result, the truth is that there is no *one* right name. There are, however, many wrong names, and naming your children wrong will set them up for a lifetime of misery (Mizeree, for girls). So please, for your sake and theirs, be careful.

new rules for antinaming

Just as there are rules for how to name your baby, there are even more rules for how not to name your baby. Use these as general guidelines while you fill out your list of things *not* to call your innocent child for the rest of his or her life.

• the rule of 3: This is the most fundamental rule for antinaming. You should employ this technique prior to your cross-check of names in this book. It is a simple technique that will help you get to your short list much faster. The Rule of 3 is this: If you can easily think of three somewhat blue words that rhyme with—or fit easily after—your child's intended first name, avoid it like the plague.

Build a chart similar to the one below to track your names. We'll get you started and you can practice by filling in the first, second, and third columns:

Name	1st	2nd	3rd	Use? (Y/N)
Tucker	F*****	Sucker	Fudpucker	N
Mulva				
Rick				
Amos				
Delores				
Mitt				
Cass				
Rawls				
Ennis				

(Continue the list with your own potential names.)

• mr. and mrs. popular: While you should certainly avoid any names that would easily allow your child to be taunted (as above), going to the opposite extreme is equally grievous. The naming safety schools of the ever popular Jennys, Joes, and Johns should be avoided for obvious reasons. But if you are still considering these types of names, let us spell it out for you.

Chances are, your child will be in school with a number of other children with the same name. As a result, teachers, friends, and enemies will by default begin to refer to your child by his or her last name. This can cause a flurry of problems, particularly if your last name is Myxlplex or the like. Additionally the reference to your child by last name will let loose an entirely new slew of independence issues that he or she will eventually have to contend with.

For instance, a gaggle of Jennys referred to only by last name, will become known independently as Peal, Plum, Floore, and Burgur. Similarly, a peck of Joes will be left to fight for independence when referred to as Smith, Jones, and Anderson. And finally, a flock of Johns will more easily be scarred, as they could be known as Thomas, Johnson, and Smallburries.

Need we say more?

• clevur speling: One of the most overlooked mistakes made by parents when attempting to give their children unique forenames is misspelling—another mistake is nepotism, but that's a different debate. There is no excuse for misspelling a name. After all, at the end of the day Genni, Jho, and Jawn will

endure the same problems as discussed in the above section, as their names are pronounced exactly the same as their popular counterparts.

But misspelled children face another, more damaging aspect in their lives—the fact that everyone will instantly think of them as a fruitcake (or as suffering from dyslexia). If you've ever met a man named Bryon or a woman named Naancie, you know what we're talking about. Naturally if you've only met Bryon and Naancie socially, you'll have no reason to question their personalities. In fact, you may grow to like Bryon and/or Naancie—until you find yourself spending a weekend with them at a business conference or trade show. Trust us, the moment you find yourself walking down the aisles of the conference hall next to the clearly labeled "Bryon" or "Naancie," the looks that their name tags will ensure will bring your relationship into question.

When naming, always run a spell check.

• boys with the boys, girls with the girls: What better way to confuse your child's sexual identity than by mixing genders? Whoever came up with this idea in the first place was a genius. Clearly thinking ahead to the child's college days (perhaps one too many drinks, a new breakup, and a comfortable same-sex shoulder to cry on), the first parents to name their boy Sue or their daughter Sol were way ahead of their time.

Mixing genders in names is second to none when it comes to what *not* to name your baby. There is debate that if a parent (or parents) want to bamboozle a child and his or her role in future relationships, mixing genders in names is actually

The Most Unpopular Names of the 1900s

The argument could be made that there are technically more unpopular names than these, but this is about as bad as it gets. They're listed from most unpopular to most popular, but according the the the Social Security Administration, they are the top 10 of the bottom 1,000 names used. As these names have been put out to pasture for over a hundred years, you would be wise to consider avoiding them as well.

Boys
Marco
Janis
Isom
Herman
Henri
Gino
Gardner
Ennis
Elgin
Darrel

Girls
Zoila
Virgil
Tressa
Rossie
Norene
Mossie
Modesta
Margit
Lempi
Kittie

more effective than simply dressing your boy in a pink, slip-on number, or potty training my gal Sol to pee standing up.

If you hope to blur the lines, go for it!

• movie mania: Pop culture rules the world. Everyone has fantasies of their life mimicking the lives of those characters they see on the big screen. A little fantasy is a good thing (and is great in the bedroom, which is probably what lead to your buying this book in the first place). However, parents who load their children with the responsibility of carrying on the name of a blockbuster are doing a disservice to the wee ones—not to mention to themselves, considering the licensing issues that could arise with the film studios.

All we ask is that you think ahead. How will little Morpheus feel when he loses a simple game of dodgeball because he can't jump in slow motion to avoid a slammer? And what about little Amidala? How do you think she'll feel when she realizes that the planet she rules over is really just a trailer park in Boise? If you're not sold yet, let us finally paint the picture of a young pair of brothers, Bo and Luke. The boys get their driver's licenses and ready their red sports car to race the local authorities. Chances are, their inability to slide through an open window effortlessly will be just enough for Ennis to cuff them and send them up the river. (Of course, they might get out early with good behavior.)

• reverse assimilation: There is something to be said about multiculturalism in naming. But unless you are cross-cultural parents, don't cross cultures. There is a reason that no WASPs are named Shaniqwa, no Jews are named Mohhamed, no African Americans are named Wong, no Asian Americans are named Irving, and so forth. Certainly there may be exceptions to the rule—Tiger Woods sounds pretty good—but for the most part, your name should reflect your culture. Not someone else's.

• they're inanimate objects for a reason: Ever since the 1900s inanimate objects have taken their place in the culture of naming in most industrialized nations. In short: Cole, Ash, and Oyl generally all contribute greatly to global warming. Naming your child after a part of our ecosystem is fine—as long as that part is not responsible for increasing the world output of carbon (monoxide, dioxide, or any other kind).

While in his youth, little Steele may feel cool for a while when he's into trains and flatbed loaders. Young Chromium may have a sound youth as she strives to be as shiny as Daddy's new Chevy rims. But as they age, their clever names will instantaneously dictate their futures. Steele will naturally take his position in life on a basic cable daytime soap opera, and Chromium may find herself inexplicably drawn to her high school chemistry teacher (as he will elementally be able to explain her innermost thoughts and feelings).

Inanimate objects are simply that. Leave them be.

• overanimated:
On the opposite end of the animate spectrum are those names that reflect objects that do have life within them. These words, typically used as nouns by most beings on planet Earth, have of late been mistaken as proper names by new and confused parents. Again, objects, whether animate or inanimate, are not to be used to name children. If your imagination is stifled by the fact that we have just eliminated twelve of your final thirteen options, here's the reality.

A typical conversation in the presence of animately named children may go as follows:

PARENT: Okay, kids, look out for that dog. We don't know if he's friendly.

DAWG: What? I'm a good kid.

PARENT: Not you, Dawg. That pit bull over there by the birch.

BIRCH: Aaaaaah! Mommy, get the dog away from me!

DAWG: I didn't touch her! Look. . . . Ha, ha. I can see that dog's johnson.

JOHNSON: See what dog, Dawg?

And so forth. Please stop the madness.

• city search:
City naming can be traced back to the early Roman Empire. At that time, there was more land in need of names than babies, and so cities were named after heroes,

villains, and conquerors. In the early 1970s actors named Dakota began popping up in the farmlands of Nebraska. Soap stars named Cheyenne appeared across all three major networks. And D'Nile was no longer just a river in Egypt.

The actual turning point (when people began to be named after cities, rather than vice versa) has yet to be pinpointed, but it seems to fall somewhere between Richard Nixon naming his dog after a board game and Gordon Sumner naming himself a verb. Trust us, the best city names have already been spent. Washington, Lincoln, and Jefferson have played their roles in history. Avoid setting your child up for a lifetime of mimicry with a more popular city name, and a lifetime of misery with a more unique city name (e.g., Wichita, Reno, or Sarasota). There's absolutely no hope.

• it's the twenty-first century: move on!

Old people are the best. Really, their wrinkly skin, their bad breath, their endless stories. All of these elements add up to a barrel of laughs (and a night of adventure!). Old people deserve to be heard. They've been through a lot more than we will ever see. In as much as they have earned our respect, they have also earned the right to be named as old people. You know the names: Murray, Irving, and Ethel.

Go right now to any rest home in your neighborhood and ask for Harry, Eugene, or Marvin. Odds are that you'll have to come up with a last name since they'll have at least two or three of each. These are the Mr. and Mrs. Popular names of our elders. And what little baby wants to be named after an old person? Names like these belong inherently to the elderly and should not be borrowed or otherwise used by anyone not retired and/or on Social Security.

• for the love of god: Biblical names have always been of use to new parents looking to define their children's personalities. Jesus, Mary, and Joseph have always been "popular" names in Mexico and the Bible Belt. However, the Solomons, Cains, and even Abels should all be put to rest. Leave these names alone. Think of it this way:

You're at the airport and raise your sign to get the attention of the client you are supposed to be picking up from Los Angeles. He's a caterer's assistant and you've never met him. All you know is that his name is Jesus. You continue to hold your sign. A few people even drop coins at your feet. Suddenly security arrives and three large officers escort you (and the Hare Krishnas) from the lobby. All this in the name of religion. Avoid the controversy.

• shop at the mall, not the nursery: One of the more disturbing naming trends of the century is *branding*. It is bad enough that with the advent of TiVo®, primetime product placement is at an all-time high, but the Social Security Administration actually recorded several new Timberlands, Luckys, and Armanis in recent years. If you are going to go to the trouble of advertising for a product through the name of your child, you might as well benefit from it as best you can. Use the following strategy:

• Spend some time researching the agency that represents the brand name you have in mind.

- Contact the agency and ask for the senior media strategist.
- Write a letter that indicates your intention to help the company build their brand through infant naming.
- Propose a win-win profit sharing opportunity that suggests if the company agrees to pay for the child's college education, you will in turn pay the company 10 percent of the child's annual income, for the life of the child, paid annually, on a mutually approvable biannual accounting basis.
- If negotiations ensue, suggest that if you as parents ever give up your option on the child, rights to the infant will revert to the company in perpetuity throughout the universe.

• sweet emotion: When it comes to the new rules of antinaming, there is no worse sin committed than that of vanity—or Hope, Joy, and Despair, for that matter. There is a time and a place for emotion, and neither coincides with the occasion of naming a child. The primary contention is simply this: Pigeonholing your child to live up to a specific emotion will lead to years of confusion. If you disagree, you'd best convert your child's college savings into a flexible medical savings account to pay for the decades of therapy your child will be sure to endure as she delves into her psyche to figure out why she's a forty-eight-year-old Virgin.

just don't do it: the list

You choose your child's name based on all kinds of criteria, not the least of which is a name's meaning. The unfortunate reality is, despite the fact that a select few of you know that Jonah means "dove" or "peaceful one," when anyone else hears that name, they instantly recognize it as "the guy who was eaten by a whale," or "the kid who set Tom Hanks up to meet Meg Ryan at the top of the Empire State Building."

As a result—and in your best interests—the actual historical definition of a name is not present in this book. Instead, you'll find the *virtual* definition—that is to say, the meaning that the majority of the population will assume upon hearing your son's name is Ajax, Braun, or Cosmo (a strong cleaning agent, a rather absorbent paper product, or the underwear model on *Seinfeld*).

It is highly recommended that you check this list to see if any of junior's potential names appear on it. If an exception to the rule appears next to the name, be sure that you meet all available criteria before moving forward with it. Good luck, and please, choose wisely.

boys' names

Abba (AH-buh or AA-ba) Mostly blond-haired, blue-eyed pop group from Denmark or Sweden, or one of those Aryan nations. Avoid use unless last name is Imma (in which case the child's name would mean "Father, Mother" and would buy the kid some leeway—at least in Hebrew school, or Chiquitita (in which case the cheese factor of ABBA's music would be cancelled out by the self-deprecating, self-titled hit song of the same name).

Abbot (AA-butt) Dim-witted, overweight sidekick. Neither this name nor its variation (see also Abba) should be used outside of Jerusalem or the walls of an area populated by men committed to a mute life of celibacy.

Aceley (ACE-lee) A kung fu action star whose gimmick is wearing white face paint

The Most Unpopular Names of the 1910s

As these names clearly reflect the idea of an agricultural society shifting into an industrialized nation, you would be wise to consider avoiding them as well.

Boys
Wylie
Winton
Valentin
Simeon
Silvio
Rueben
Roswell
Rose
Reid
Pierre

Girls
Thyra
Susana
Paulina
Maryjane
Macie
Leonore
Laurine
Katy
Imelda
Elta

Source: Social Security Administration

and platform moon boots. This word should be used only as an adverb, e.g., "He rocks aceley!" but never as a name unless the intention is to ruin the infant's life from the get-go.

Acheron (AA-ke-ren) One of the five rivers of Hell. Come on. Please.

Achilles (uh-KILL-eez) Annoying ligament of one's heel that hurts anytime one thinks of it. Not recommended for children, though it is highly recommended for dogs—particularly those that are being trained to stay close to their owners on walks.

Ackerley (ACK-er-lee) A copse of oak trees. As a general rule, names ending in "ly," "lee," or "ley" should be avoided at all cost, especially for boys. Also steer clear of names that imply a startled interjection. See also Ajou, Chumchum, and Uzi.

Acton (ACK-tun) Oak town. Also, treading the boards, pretending to be someone else in front of a large audience.

Adaire (uh-DARE) Oak tree settlement. Enough with the trees. See Arbor.

Adam (AA-dam) An irritating child who insists on being first in everything—genetically, chronologically, and alphabetically. Also, a famous ant.

Admiral (AD-mi-ral) One who manages a weekly voyage of '80s guest stars as they travel to such locations as Puerto

Vallarta, Cabo San Lucas, and (during sweeps weeks) Alaska. Exceptions to the rule: if your last name is Bird or Kirk.

Adolf (AY-dolf) Thin-mustached psychopath. Lunatic. Once a popular name in Eastern block countries, Adolf quickly fell from fashion in the late '30s and early '40s. Not an option for any child.

Adonis (uh-DON-iss) Handsome youth. While the name sounds good and looks good on paper, such a name implies a certain level of narcissism that no child can bear. See also Jesus, Einstein, and Zeus.

Aeneas (uh-KNEE-us) Area responsible for the final stages of digestion. Rhymes with "heinous." There are no exceptions for any names rhyming with "heinous."

Aeon (EE-yawn) Forever and a day. Beyond eternity. Your child's name will last longer than he does. And if that doesn't convince you, then just think of the irony of your offspring's epitaph.

Aesop (EE-sahp) Writer of morals. Exception to the rule: if your last name is Sphables.

Aire (ayr) The Democratic Republic of the Congo. However, virtual meaning is rather unstable, much like the political climate of the region. Avoid use until at least after the next coup.

Ajax (AY-jacks) A sturdy, granulated bathroom-cleaning agent. Exeption to the rule: blue-collar families with type A personalities.

Ajou (ah-JHOO) Beef bouillon served in a dish over meat sandwich. Also, the sound a sneeze makes. Additionally, when your child is summoned by name (e.g., in class) teacher may seem anti-Semitic.

Alastair (AL-eh-stir) Strong but aged man who typically speaks with a British accent and announces "Previously on . . ." for long, boring public programming.

Albany (ALL-ba-knee) The state capital of New York. Also, a city on a white hill. Today the name suggests a not-so-white hill (environmentally speaking).

Alcander (al-CAN-der) Blatantly blunt. Thoroughly candid. Also, extremely attracted to sheep. Exception to the rule: Bouloukos or Damakis.

Alejandro (al-uh-HAN-dro) A handsome pool boy shared by the Stepford wives.

Algernon (AL-ger-non) Mentally impaired mouse befriended by character actor Cliff Robertson.

Aliah (ah-LEE-ah) A Jewish prayer. Honor bestowed upon uncles, aunts, cousins, siblings, parents, and grandparents of a bar mitzvah boy (or bat mitzvah girl) before the Torah reading and schnapps and herring.

Amadeus (ah-ma-DAY-us) Subject of an '80s pop hit by Falco.

See also Falco. Use of such a name in any circumstance risks the child's growing up to wear tight vinyl clothing and speak unintelligible English. Exception to the rule: child prodigies. However, pianists should be aware that their peers might think them grandiose because of a long dead, highly esteemed piano man with the same name.

Amen (ah-MEN) Time to eat. Unless the child is bound for a monastery, the confusion that will ensue anytime the child hears a prayer is not worth the religious implications.

Anakin (AN-uh-kin) Egotistical Jedi. Though there is no historical case proving that an Anakin can overcome, use of such a name will generally say more about the parent than the child (i.e., You clearly have a powerful fantasy life, and you're probably a big geek. How did you ever find anyone to bear your children?). This may lead to frequent schoolyard taunting and justifiable rebellion.

Ancelin (ANN-sell-in) Currently in the first phase of trials with the FDA. If Ancelin is approved, your child may be an affordable, noninvasive cure-all for lockjaw and tetanus. If not, he will be another unsuccessful attempt at restructuring the health care system.

Andy (ANN-dee) An uncoordinated, red-haired boy with a taste for gingham. Likely to be called Randy Andy in junior high.

Angel (AYN-gel) Keep the boy off the pole. Just keep the boy off the pole.

The Most Unpopular Names of the 1920s

As these names are clearly a reflection of a far too sober society, you would be wise to consider avoiding them as well.

Boys
Wylie
Winton
Tracy
Terrence
Rexford
Quincy
Moises
Melville
Lafayette
Ivy

Girls
Verlie
Pauline
Natalia
Michelina
Mariam
Lavera
Izetta
Hortensia
Eris
Elois

Source: Social Security Administration

Angus (ANG-guhs) Scottish breed of cow. Also, when sliced in one-pound sections and grilled over hot coals, available with a shrimp cocktail for $4.99 in Las Vegas. Exceptions to the rule: families with cowboys, ranchers, or rodeo stars.

Anthem (AN-thum) Opening ceremony at sporting events. Hymn of praise and loyalty. A child so named may be inherently motivated to stand at inopportune moments in Little League and peewee soccer matches.

Anthony/Tony (AN-doe-nee)/(DOE-nee) An Italian child ignored by fat aunts because of his long fingernails and garlic breath.

Antwaun (ANN-twahn) An urban (see also Urban) variation on Anthony. Invaluable. However, due to the recent upsurge in popularity with regard to the name Antwaun, new meanings are a dime a dozen.

Apache (uh-PAA-chee) U.S. military attack helicopter. Also, a tribe of Native Americans who suffered great losses during their Texan wars of 1845 to 1850. Exception to the rule: Democrats living in Fort Worth.

Apollo (uh-PAHL-oh) The Greek god of healing, light, and truth. The bad guy who beat Rocky in *Rocky*. A child so named will be disliked by most Italian Americans until he begins part two of his life—at which time he will make friends with the Italian Americans and even train them to fight large, Mohawk-wearing boxers with worse names.

Aramis (AAR-a-miss) A masculine scent with a blend of spices, leather, moss, sandalwood, and clove. Recommended for evening wear, not for newborns.

Arbor (ARE-bore) Shady resting place. This name may be used by overweight children, or infants with particularly gargantuan proboscises.

Arby (ARE-bee) Maker of thinly sliced, fine meat sandwiches. A child bearing such a name may gain a lot of attention two or three times a year from people asking for five favors for five dollars. Alternatively, child will frequently be called upon to explain which sauce is white and which is red.

Argus (ARE-gus) Giant with one hundred eyes. According to Greek mythology, half of the eyes suffered from insomnia. Additionally, after performing an infamous act of kidnapping, Argus was slain, and his eyes were distributed evenly onto the feathers of a peacock. This is not the kind of story you want for your child.

Army (ARE-mee) A large group of men and women sent into battle at the whim of a public official—regardless of justification, evidence, and sexual orientation. Child will be great at taking orders, but not a particularly free thinker.

Arrow (AA-row) A pointed stick. Also, a "gas-saving" model of Plymouth introduced into the United States in the late '60s. Child's seat may stick when reclined.

Ash (aash) Flaky carbon by-product of fire. If you are going to the lengths of naming your child after the elements that signify a particular era in American history, you might as well get up to speed. The industrial era is over. It is now the age of information. Pentium, Silicon, and Apple are more current than Ash. See also Cole.

Asher (AA-shur) One who is a flaky carbon by-product of fire.

Ashes (AASH-iz) Many flaky carbon by-products of fire.

Athens (ATH-enz) The capital city of Greece, and also, a nice place to visit in Georgia. Child may be plagued by an overly greasy hairstyle, a thick Southern drawl, and the distinct smell of loukanika.

Atlantic (at-LAN-tick) Large, deep body of ocean water separating North America from its friends and enemies.

Atlantis (at-LAN-tiss) A dead city at the bottom of the ocean. See also Atlantic. A real winner when it comes to naming, particularly if your child will be a swimmer.

Attila (uh-TILL-uh) A hun. Grog-drinking, meat-eating, fur-bearing thug. For visual, picture Governor Arnold Schwarzenegger in *Conan the Barbarian*.

Aubrey (AWE-bree) Teutonic ruler of the elves. Unless your infant's cauliflower ear remains pointed after his third month, consider changing his name. Other negative implications to keep in mind are that the feature-film trilogy responsible for making elves popular has already been released on DVD and will be passé by the time your child reaches puberty.

Audi (OW-dee) High-performance extension of the penis. Also, slang for leaving, going, moving on. If you are considering this name, you should do the same.

Austin (AWE-stun) The capital of Texas, and the bionic man.

Auto (AWE-toe) Not manual. Also, a circular or piston-driven engine that creates energy when a spark ignites a combination of gasoline and air. Exceptions to the rule: if your last name is Benz, Ford, or von Baron.

Avon (AY-von) A popular makeup brand with ads all over TV in the early '50s. Known for its broad coverage, bright colors, and army of saleswomen racing a bunch of pastel-colored Cadillacs. A great name for a boy!

Axel (AX-uhl) Screw-up Michigan detective working primarily in Beverly Hills, California. Child may be plagued by a hyena-like laugh.

Badger (BAA-jer) Angry, furry varmint known for its violent temperament.

Baja (BAH-ha) Sliver of land off the mainland coast of Mexico. Hideaway for celebrities and rock stars. Exception to the rule: if you dream of a child who knows how to get you backstage.

Balthazar (BAL-thu-czar) One of the original three kings who visited upon Mary and Joseph sometime in the late winter. History is uncertain as to whether Balthazar carried and delivered the gold, frankincense, or myrrh. Exceptions to the rule: if your last name is Gold, Frankincense, or Myrrh.

Banjo (BAN-joe) Stringed instrument generally played in a duel prior to departing on weekend river trip in the South.

Barclay (BAR-klee) Meadow of birch trees.

Barney (BAR-knee) Large purple dinosaur adored by children, despised by parents.

Bartleby (BAR-tuhl-bee) Often mistaken for a cheap whiskey or circus clown. Exception to the rule: if your last name is Jones and young Bartleby has two daddies.

Basil (BAA-zul) A green, leafy herb generally wilting if not used within three days of purchase.

Beavis (BEE-vus) Along with Butt-Head, the animated television stars blamed for many double-wides going up in flames. Their rude behavior led to the cancellation of their television series, but their legacy lives on through unlicensed and poorly produced T-shirts sold in truck stops and minimarts along the interstate.

Beethoven (BAY-tove-in) A large and mischievous Saint Bernard.

Benjamin (BEN-ja-min) Action of Rastafarian after inhaling the sensimilla.

Bliss (bliss) A temporary state of ecstasy usually characterized by wide eyes and an ear-to-ear grin. A more permanent condition often goes hand-in-hand with members of cults and large missionary-driven religious organizations.

Bond (bahnd) A chemical agent that serves to hold together various materials. Also, a loose but attractive agent from the UK who is known for his sexy demeanor and gimmicky technology.

Boris (BORE-iss) A short, Russian spy who has an affinity for lanky Soviet models. Child may be plagued by frequent nightmares involving both moose and squirrels. Exceptions to the rule: if your last name is Karloff or Wazngoodenoff.

Brady (BRAY-dee) One who actually gets along well with stepsiblings and stepparents. Warning: Brady brothers may have an attraction to Brady sisters (and mothers, when the cameras stop rolling).

Braedon (BRAY-dn) Activity of winding three bunches of hair together usually undertaken by teenage girls while speaking endlessly about what they were "like" after who said what to whom.

Brandon (BRAN-don) A Vermont town famous for birdhouses. The child will likely be described as a delicate boy with large jowls.

Braun (brawn) A hefty, absorbent paper towel. Also, a supplier of travel accessories best known for its razors and nose hair trimmers.

Brendan (BREN-den) Fighter of mummies. Child's appearance on *People* magazine's short list of the sexiest men will be short-lived.

Brian (BREYE-on) Mistaken Messiah. Around 1 BC Brian was accidentally vilified by Roman soldiers looking for a different Jew. On the positive side, your child may always look on the bright side.

Briley (BREYE-lee) The rough texture of parasites found on the underside of ships' hulls and the top side of whales' median notches.

Brittyn (BRIH-ton) The once powerful United Kingdom, whose philosophy of "divide and conquer" made it the smallest and most powerful island in the world, at least until George W. Bush was elected. Last-name exceptions to the rule include Ie and Ish.

Bryce (brice) A canyon in southern Utah.

Buckaroo (buhck-a-REW) A hero resembling Peter Weller, who did battle with an army of alien forces all named John, across the eighth dimension. Exception to the rule: if your last name is Banzai.

Bud (bud) Springtime precursor to a flower or leaf. Organic substance used initially in high school to heighten understanding of Pink Floyd's *Dark Side of the Moon*. Exception to the rule: if you want your child to be surrounded by a lot of giggling every time someone says his name in college.

Bullock (BULL-uck) A castrated bull. See also Angus.

The Most Unpopular Names of the 1930s

As these names were invented by women in flapper attire and men who drank moonshine, you would be wise to consider avoiding them as well.

Boys
Williams
Stan
Smith
Sherwin
Reece
Randal
Norval
Newman
Matt
Jarvis

Girls
Zona
Santos
Romona
Mayme
Marvel
Jerline
Jamie
Idell
Esta
Dorine

Source: Social Security Administration

Bus (bus) Vehicle used for public transportation, generally dirty, greasy, and undesirable for use.

Busta (BUS-tah) A rhymer, a rapper, and a candlestick maker.

Buster (BUS-ter) Caucasian form of Busta.

Butch (butch) A skinny boy with a big Adam's apple, or a short, fat woman with a crew cut and a penchant for driving muscle cars.

Cache (cash) Money. Also, computer memory used to continually update one's operating system.

Caesar (SEE-zer) Salad ordered most often on first dates with a Diet Coke. Also, wearer of wreaths, one who is stabbed in the back.

Caleb (KAY-lub) Biblical, yes, but in this day and age, very soap opera-ish. Also, a waxy chocolate substitute.

Cameron (CAM-run) Technology that allows you to capture all of your best memories in photographic form.

Captain (KAP-ten) One who commands a starship where no *man* has gone before. Exceptions to the rule: if your last name is Kirk or Antennille.

Carew (kuh-REW) A smaller, less crescent-shaped nut that is not as salty, not as tasty, and not as popular as its larger, better cousin.

Carlos (CAR-lohss) Used for maximum effect when juxtaposed with a non-Hispanic surname, e.g., Carlos Bernstein, Carlos McDougal, Carlos Romanoff. Also a good name for a foraging canine.

Carmel (kar-MEHL) Popular beachfront community generally inhabited by former celebrities. Sweet and chewy substance added to macchiato. As a general rule, best to avoid the matching of names and foodstuffs. See also Sugar.

Carson (CAR-sun) A child who is popular for no known reason.

Carter (CAR-ter) A jovial peanut farmer or cable TV carpenter who measures once and cuts twice.

Caruso (ka-REW-so) One who is lost at sea.

Carvel (kar-VEHL) An annoying ice-cream maker whose franchises have been pegged to the East Coast.

Casper (KAS-per) A friendly ghost. A homosexual albino.

Cedric (SAID-rick) A Celtic chieftain, or an entertainer.

Champion (CHAM-pee-uhn) A winner or a spark plug. Let the kid earn this title himself; otherwise, you open the door to major entitlement issues.

Chanse (chance) An opportunity. A slight possibility, e.g., "There is a Chanse that your son is gay."

Charger (CHAR-jur) One who plays football in San Diego. Also, one that clips on to a battery and provides power.

Charles/Chuck (charlz)/(chuck) Another name reminiscent of vomit. Not a good name for the banana rhyming song either.

Chase (chace) To run after. In dogs, to blindly spin in circles to get to that pointy thing that keeps showing up in their periphery.

Chevrolet (shev-row-LAY) General Motors vehicle that may be recalled at some point in its life. Exceptions to the rule: if your last name is Citation, Motors, or Cavalier.

Chip-wa (CHIP-wah) Sound made by martial artist prior to delivering a deadly blow.

Christian (KRIS-chun) Reserved for gentiles.

Christopher (KRIS-toe-fer) One who sails the ocean blue. Also, odd boy whose best friends are stuffed bears and tiny pigs.

Chumchum (hmm-HMM) Sound made when clearing one's throat.

Cleveland (KLEEV-lend) City often mistaken as the capital city of Ohio. See also Columbus. Exception to the rule: if you aspire to raise a cardsharp.

Cody (CO-dee) A meth-lab-running, strip-club-at-lunch kind of guy.

Colby (KOLE-bee) A mild cheddar cheese from the woods of New England.

Cole (KOLE) A black, organic substance often used as barbeque fuel.

Colin (CAH-lin) A cancer-prone part of the body near the rectum made famous by Katie Couric.

Colonel (KER-nul) Crunchy remains of unheated popcorn. Also, leader of a ragtag troupe of former army experts including Mr. T. Exceptions to the rule: if your last name is Blake, Potter, or (last-middle or hyphenated combination) George Peppard.

Columbus (co-LUM-bus) The capital city of Ohio. See also Cleveland. One who *discovered* America . . . right after the Native Americans. Exceptions to the rule: if your last name is Ohio, Day, or Sailedtheoceanblue.

The Most Unpopular Names of the 1940s

As these names were clearly the result of a depressed nation about to go to war, you would be wise to consider avoiding them as well.

Boys
Verl
Marshal
Lyn
Kenney
Hilario
Eusibio
Epifanio
Emoch
Diego
Chad

Girls
Rona
Nicole
Nancie
Myrtis
Merlene
Marianna
Linnea
Kathlyn
Jocelyn
Isabell

Source: Social Security Administration

Connor (CON-er) One who swindles lunch money from the other kids. Also, one who will rise to save the world from the machines.

Cosmo (KAHZ-moe) The big-haired, crazy one from *Seinfeld*.

Count (kownt) Purple-skinned, white-fanged Muppet whose OCD manifests in fanatic numerology that rarely explores numbers past twenty.

Coy (koy) A mutated, large goldfish.

Coyote (kei-OH-tee) One who is unable to trap quick birds for consumption. One with a penchant for pre-Costco warehouse products.

Crispin (KRIS-pen) Lunatic actor who can kick . . . high.

Crosby (KRAHZ-bee) Long-haired singer of harmonies, generally known for drug abuse.

Daaron (DARE-on) To encourage one to do something really, really stupid, like jumping off the roof to see if one can fly.

Dagger (DAA-ger) A long, sharp knife most often used to stab people after they trustingly turn their backs to you.

Dajuan (da-WHAN) Spanish pronunciation of "the one," e.g., "Yes, Officer, that's Dajuan who stole my purse."

Dakota (duh-COAT-uh) Twin states separated by an imaginary line. Also, daytime television star who, after unknowingly marrying his sister, drove off a cliff (tried to get a job in feature films), and then returned after plastic surgery to exact revenge on his stepfather.

Dalton (DAWL-ten) Pseudoclassy. Dalton's brothers and sisters will be Bentley, Tremayne, and Ashlee.

Damarcius (da-MAR-shus) Located west of the fens and south of the mountains, this area is swampy and host to malarial mosquitos.

Damien (DAY-me-in) A head-spinning child of the devil. Also, a priest who administered to lepers. Exceptions to the rule: if your last name is Thorn, Omentwo, or Finalconflict.

Dandray (DAN-dray) A flaky scalp condition often treated with medicated shampoos.

Daniel/Dan (DAN-yul)/(dan) Just call him the adlib boy "Dan, Dan the (fill in the blank) man . . ."

D'ante (DAHN-tay) Creator of fiery infernos.

Darth (dahrth) Treacherous father. Child's heavy breathing will make him an outcast and a perfect recruit for cults or other, lesser-known evil empires.

David (DAY-vid) A stoic boy with an unusually large hand who enjoys just standing around without any clothes on. The little guy who is always ready to take on the big guys.

Dax (daks) A strong industrial cleanser able to get out the toughest biohazard stains.

DeAaron (dee-AIR-on) What one must do when the temperature inside reaches ungodly heights: put DeAaron. Also, what one must be sure to do before descending under the watery depths in a submarine.

De-Arse (dee-ARSS) (British) One's rear end.

DeeWayne (dee-WAYN) The love child of the toughest cowboy who ever lived and the prissy girl from *Grease*.

Del Roy (DELL-roy) Likely to pick up a strange-looking hitch-hiker in the Nevada desert who turns out to be either a reclusive billionaire or a space alien.

DeLawrence (duh-LAW-rinse) It's de-lightful, it's de-lovely, it's DeLawrence!

De-Lewis (dee-LEW-iss) What the Multiple Dystrophy Society will do when they choose a new Labor Day telethon host.

DellBert (DELL-bert) Unlike his brother, who found success in technology, DellBert continued his career in animal husbandry on the family farm.

De-Mario (dee-MAREE-o) To remove that very special essence of lasagna from a person, car, or house.

Demarkus (duh-MAR-cuss) To delineate by a boundary. Also, to swear under one's breath, preferably at a teacher or family member.

DeMichael (duh-MIKE-ull) Why is Michael such a dumbass? Why?

De-Morris (dee-MAW-russ) A person strongly opposed to finicky house pets.

Denim Levi (DEN-im LEAVE-eye) A textile magnate unable to wear comfortable blue garments.

Dent (dent) A folded or flattened surface. This child's oddly misshapen cranium will be the hit of the junior high school yearbook signing party.

De-Ole (dee-OLE) Similar to "ye olde." Often used by grand-pas talking about a move from the past. "I'll show him De-Ole one-two punch."

DeRail (duh-RAYLE) An interrupter. His citizenship marks will never be better than *Unsatisfactory*.

Derek (DARE-ick) Machine consisting of cables and pullies, used for moving heavy objects.

Derringer (DARE-inn-jer) A small, underpowered gun used by cheats and cowards.

Desert (DEH-zert) A place where nothing can live but cactuses, bugs, and snakes. Name will often be misspelled and mistaken for its sweeter, postdinner cousin.

Dewight (duh-WHITE) A happy name adopted when a child can't say his *L*s.

Dewrangee (duh-RANGE-ee) To make crazy, insane, or just plain nuts.

Dex (decks) An accessible know-it-all in the West.

Dicy (DIE-cee) Unstable and tentative. Also, associated with fuzzy mirror ornaments. May speak in nursery rhymes.

Diego (dee-EGG-oh) A fabulous zoo in Southern California. Exception to the rule: if your last name is Rivera and you want people to wonder if your son is heir to a famous painter.

Digger (DIH-ger) Nickname of Jock Ewing's business rival, and Miss Ellie's former love, on the '70s series *Dallas*. A great name for a dog, cemetery manager, or miner.

Dillinger (DILL-in-jer) Midwestern criminal who was best known to the American public through his pictures on post office Wanted posters. Not a great name for a family in the banking industry.

Dionysus (di-uh-NIGH-sus) The Greek god of wine, fertility, and drama. To protect him from the wrath of Zeus's wife, Dionysus was raised as a girly god by his caretakers.

The Most Unpopular Names of the 1950s

As these names were utilized at a time when men were men and sheep were scared, you would be wise to consider avoiding them as well.

Boys
Vernell
Truman
Shirley
Murphy
Melton
Maxwell
Lynwood
Leander
Lannie
Hosea

Girls
William
Venita
Tammi
Ruthann
Neil
Lise
Letitia
Corine
Caron
Venus

Source: Social Security Administration

Dirk (durk) A sharp, short Scottish sword. In the same league as Bruce, Lance, and Steve.

D'Loaf (duh-LOAF) To make a peanut butter and jelly sandwich, first take two slices from D'Loaf of bread.

Dock (dahk) A place on the bay where you sit and watch the tide roll away. Child will become tired of being asked, "What's up?"

Dominic (DOM-en-ick) Failed tile game played with one rectangular piece. Development was quickly halted when Dominic's cousin realized that the game was more fun when played with multiple tiles.

Donl (DON-ull) A wealthy, conceited real estate baron with bad hair, best known for firing employees.

D'Orr (duh-ORR) Often confused with "door," as in "Don't let the D'Orr hit you in the arse on your way out."

Dragon (DRA-gen) A mythical beast that breathes fire and kills noble knights to steal their loot. Also associated with severe halitosis and long fingernails.

Drakkar (DRACK-ar) Popular '80s cologne effective in covering the smell of smoke or marijuana.

Dred (dread) Sibling of fear and loathing. Also, rolled, matted hairdo that makes use of cow manure.

Dude (dewd) The tragic subject of the Aerosmith song who will have gender identity issues. Will grow up to become a valet parking attendant.

Duffin (DUFF-in) Hairdresser affectionately known as Muffin by his significant other. Aquaman.

Duke (dewk) A badass gunslinger. Also, a fluffy ruler in the UK. Teachers will find his cocksure swagger, Liberace style of dress, and tendency to call the other children "pilgrim" annoying and distracting.

Dull (duhl) Not the sharpest knife in the drawer. A child never invited to parties. An also-ran in the 2000 presidential election and a spokesperson for a medical problem that men refuse to talk about.

Dylan (DILL-un) A hard-boiled Welsh poet who drank himself to death; a whiny '60s folk singer.

E Ray (EE-ray) Advertised in the back of comic books, E Ray vision allows young boys to see through women's dresses.

Eagle (EE-gull) A symbol of freedom for the United States. The top rank of the Boy Scouts. Unfortunately a name that is reserved for Native Americans.

Earl (erl) A needlefish and an English nobleman's title. Sounds like "hurl," which is synonymous with regurgitation.

Earnest (UR-nest) Honest. Sincere. Exception to the rule: if you feel it is important, you may be Earnest.

Ebenezer (ebb-uh-KNEES-er) Miserly curmudgeon who grudgingly accepts the joy of Christmas. God bless us every one!

Einstein (EIN-stine) Clever one with wild hair. One may never live up to this name and will always be subject to comments such as, "Nice shot, Einstein," or "Who knows the answer, Einstein?"

Elder (ELL-der) Will get far more respect from the other children due to his long white beard and furrowed brow.

Elgin (ELL-jin *or* ell-JIN) Scottish lord who either stole the Parthenon marbles or spirited them to England for "safe-keeping." Also used by police with Latin suspects: "Put down Elgin and come out with your hands up."

Elijah (ee-LIE-juh) An actor typecast for life as a ring-bearing hobbit.

Elmer (ELL-murr) A white glue consumed by preschool children and used to fix just about any household mishap that doesn't require duct tape. Destined to chase, but never catch, rabbits.

Elroy (ELL-roy) In the absence of his parents, will be raised by the robot maid. His only friend is destined to be his dog, Rastro.

Elvis (ELL-viss) There is only one Elvis.

Elvoid (ELL-void) The complete absence of Elvis qualities.

Enigma (eh-NIG-ma) A puzzled child destined to spend thirteen years as a philosophy major without ever graduating college.

Eros (AIR-ohss) Short, chubby, naked baby with wings and a prayer. Tends to shoot at lonely people with a bow and arrow to inspire them to jump in bed together.

Erwin (ER-win) The phrase used when beginning the story about how the car wreck was not your fault. Usually uttered after curfew has passed. Famed hunter of amphibious reptiles.

Espin (ESS-pin) Only a sports fanatic with cable TV would consider this name for a child. Exception to the rule: if you are a professional athlete and want the guys at the network to give you a little extra coverage.

Ethan (EE-thin) A thick sweater–wearing, curly-haired college kid who smokes a lot of pot.

Eubie (YOU-bee) Someone new to speaking Black lingo.

Eugene (YOU-jeen) DNA strand believed to be responsible for math ability. Why not just give him a CPA, bow tie, and plaid polyester sport coat and be done with it?

Falco (FAAL-ko) Pop star of the '80s known for his tight pants and unintelligible English. See also Amadeus.

Farmer (FAR-mur) One who wears baggy trousers and floppy hats and has an affinity for sheep.

Farteaun (FART-tone) The musical register of one's flatulence.

Ferris (FEHR-iss) A teenager who can get away with anything. Also, bubbly, expensive water.

Fifine/Fifi (FEE-fean)/(FEE-fee) A miniature French poodle that accompanies its owner to the salon and is dyed pink for special occasions.

Flavious (FLAY-vee-us) The Roman god of tasty meals.

Flavo (FLAY-vo) The short-lived '50s cartoon mascot on the glass jar of fish bouillon cubes. A Southwestern chef's special reserve, but not quite VSOP quality.

FoFo (FO-fo) Because PoPo was already taken.

Francisco (fran-SIS-co) A sourdough lover and gay boy from the get-go. Exception to the rule: last name, Franco.

Free (free) Absolutely no charge. Better for a boy than for a girl, about whom it could easily be said that she just gives it away.

Fritz (fritss) A plump German exchange student.

Fritznel (FRITSS-nul) Schnitzel made from Fritz.

g

Gabriel (GAY-bree-el) The archangel who informed Mary of the virgin birth. Also,

The Most Unpopular Names of the 1960s

As these names were clearly invented by a society completely confused between love and war, you would be wise to consider avoiding them as well.

Boys
Truman
Tory
Tobin
Titus
Silas
Malcom
Lacy
King
Kennith
Jules

Girls
Winifred
Tamala
Sherrill
Romna
Maricela
Darcie
Casandra
Blanche
Tommie
Thea

Source: Social Security Administration

the van-driving, sunglass-wearing leader of an obscure religious sect with a compound in the desert.

Gage (gayj) A device that enables the measurement of air, water, and other things.

Gannon (GANN-un) A rainbow-colored artillery piece.

Garland (GAR-lund) Could become a pill-popping cross-dresser with a soaring soprano.

Garrison (GAAR-iss-un) Will annoy his friends by forcing them to stage radio variety shows in the backyard and speak incessantly about some creepy lake that no one can find on the map.

Gates (gaytz) No amount of money will make this boy attractive to women.

Gatlin (GAT-lun) A special soul food made from cat intestines.

Gavin (GA-vin) Jaunty captain who piloted a cruise full of dysfunctional singles to Acapulco every Friday night in the late '70s and early '80s.

Gaye (gay) An old name that unfortunately will no longer be associated with happy.

Gaylord (GAY-lord) Oh, who are you kidding? Why would you saddle a child with this?

General (JEN-rul) Neighbor children will lose sleep over whether your bossy child will assign them to KP.

George (jorj) The first U.S. president and a dragon slayer.

German (JER-mun) A studious and hardworking child who, not being satisfied with the size of his room, will be prone to annexing other rooms in the house.

Gideon (GI-dee-uhn) The owner of all hotel Bibles.

Gilligan (GILL-i-gun) Little buddy of a barrel-chested sailor and rumored *petit ami* of the movie star.

God (gawd) Ruler of the universe. Child may become confused when required to spell his name with an em-dash in Hebrew school.

Goody (GU-dee) His name will be called with delight by older women who smell like talcum powder.

Grant (grant) To give or acknowledge. Child may tend to have an affinity for charity or public radio stations.

Grover (GROVE-ur) A sweet, but somewhat dim-witted child with an inexplicable medical condition that causes strange blue hair growth and a croaky voice.

Gulliver (GUH-li-vur) A man who is big when others are small and small when others are big.

Gusty (GUSS-tee) Will be prone to uncontrollable and embarrassing attacks of flatulence.

Halliwell (HAL-ih-well) Will wear baby doll dresses and cause the breakup of all groups to which he belongs.

Handsome (HAN-some) Will inevitably turn when women on the corner yell, "Hello, Handsome!"

Hannibal (HAA-ni-buhl) Roman general best known for using elephants to cross the Alps. Will have a fondness for liver, fava beans, and Chianti.

Hansel (HAN-suhl) With his sister, Gretel, ate a cookie house and convinced the evil witch that they were skin and bones. First documented example of sibling eating disorders.

Happy (HAA-pee) A dwarf who will be used as an example when others are anxious, e.g., "Don't worry, be Happy!"

Harold/Harry (HAA-rolled)/(HAA-ree) Swimming at the pool, people will wonder why he's wearing a sweater vest. Likely to reach puberty earlier than the other boys.

Hauk (hawk) The unpleasant noise associated with clearing one's throat in order to collect a loogie.

Hayden (HAY-din) Don't be Hayden!

Hazelup (HAZE-ull-up) Noncaffeinated nut protein soda made popular after the granolalike bars were found to be carcinogenic.

Hector (HECK-tur) A garbage collector. Also, the son of King Priam and Queen Hecuba of Troy, and leader of the kingdom's forces during the Trojan War. His death at the hands of Achilles foretold the fall of Troy. A common name for Mexican taxi drivers.

Henri (on-REE) Ornery and cantankerous French child.

Henry (HEN-ree) Ornery and cantankerous chicken.

Herschel (HER-shull) A great American chocolate bar, with or without nuts. Likely to be overweight and have chronic acne.

Hiram (HIGH-rum) Common name for a hired man or an indentured servant. Definitely not as glamorous as, and certainly more blister-making than, being a kept boy.

Holt (holt) To capture or keep tight.

Honor (ON-ur) The inevitable subject of joking by adolescent males. "Now, where were you last night? Honor?"

Horace (HOR-us) A quality of voice most notable after a particularly close football game, a street fight, or a bad throat cold.

Horatio (hor-AY-show) One who is always excited for entertainment.

Huggy Bear (HU-ghee-bare) A '70s television-show character best remembered for snitching on his friends and having poor taste in clothing. See also Vinyl.

Hunter (HUN-ter) An orange vest– and camouflage-wearing boy who doesn't catch and release.

Hutch (hutch) A kitchen cupboard or a '70s policeman played by David Soul. Or was that Starsky? See Starsky.

Hyman (HI-man) A casual male greeting. Brother to Cherry.

Ian (EE-an) A really long time.

Ichabod (ICK-uh-bod) May be a thin, awkward schoolteacher chased by headless horsemen.

Ideal (EYE-deel) An online bargain. Radial keratotomy negotiation. Common placard in a used car lot.

Iggy (IGG-ee) Fine if your child is a little green monster.

Igor (EE-gore) One-eyed lab assistant whose key attribute is hand wringing. Effective if your goal is to see child employed at a glove-manufacturing plant.

Ima (EYE-mah) Will be perpetually subject to the childhood game "I know you are, but what am I?"

Indiana (in-dee-AN-uh) Rugged alter ego of an otherwise boorish academic anthropologist.

Irelan (EYER-lan) Neighbor of Englan, Wale, and Scotlan.

Ivan (EYE-vin) Gimme-grabbee child whose only goal is the fulfillment of his own desires.

j

Jabari (juh-BAR-ee) A new safari-themed board game for the whole family!

The Most Unpopular Names of the 1970s

As these names obviously originated from a nation waking from a ten-year drug-induced coma, you would be wise to consider avoiding them as well.

Boys
Tucker
Thurman
Samson
Russ
Quintin
Lars
Gus
Garret
Gabe
Ezequiel

Girls
Roxanna
Robbie
Petra
Pearl
Nicki
Leilani
Kylie
Kenyatta
Cherise
Anika

Source: Social Security Administration

Jack (jak) A dashing polo player who is likely to have only one eye. Also, a popular name for donkeys.

Jackson (JAK-sun) Boy child of a cheese maker in Monterey, California.

Jacob (JAY-kub) A well-to-do ladder retailer.

Jaguar (JAG-ewe-arr) Fast and incredibly handsome, but known to be very unreliable.

Jai (high) The least fabulous of the Fab Five.

Jake (jayk) Perpetual high schooler whom all the freshman girls will love and all the freshman boys will be convinced is a narc. Subject to "Jake, Jake the Snake" tauntings.

Jalen (JAY-len) The act of placing a person within the confines of a penitentiary.

James/Jim (jaymz)/(jim) A thin, sticklike meat product with a shelf life of thirty-seven years. Also, the captain of a fabled starship.

Ja'mon (JAM-on) To rock in the reggae style, as in "we be Ja'mon." Also, slang for, "I agree with you wholeheartedly."

Jar (jarr) A vessel used for canning fruits, vegetables, and removed organs. Also, a member of the US Marines.

Jason (JAY-sun) A hockey-masked murderer.

Jeb (jeb) Governor best known for disenfranchised constituency and dangling chads.

Jed (jed) Hillbilly oil prospector who loved his ce-ment pond.

Jedi (JED-eye) A noble knight who compulsively plays with his Lightsaber.

Jeep (jeep) A go-anywhere type of guy. Likes to take his top off and get muddy.

Jeffrey (JEF-ree) A long-necked toy store mascot.

Jenner (JEH-ner) Decathlete with his own Wheaties box.

Jeremiah (jair-uh-MY-uh) A prophet alone, crying in the wilderness.

Jeremy (JAIR-uh-mee) One who has spoken. Yeeeeeeeeees, he did.

Jesse (JES-ee) A cowboy from the Wild, Wild West.

Jesus (JEE-zus) Star of a popular 2004 box-office smash!

Jethro (JETH-row) Pompadoured cousin to Ellie Mae. Continually victimized by Granny and her wooden spoon.

Jimmy (JIH-mee) The multicolored sprinkles on top of cupcakes, shaped like male genitalia.

Jock (johk) A sporty fellow, and Miss Ellie's wildcatter husband on the '70s series *Dallas,* who was an ardent athletic supporter.

Joe (joh) American for "coffee."

Joel (jole) A musically inclined supermodel magnet who is prone to car accidents.

John (jahn) One who purchases the services of prostitutes. Also, a toilet.

John Thomas (jahn-TAH-mus) Yet another name for the wee one.

Joplin (JOP-lun) Seventies female rocker prone to weight fluctuation and drug use.

Jordan (JOR-dun) A basketball legend, boy band has-been, and topless UK model.

Jor-El (jor-ELL) Father of Superman. Or if he wasn't, he should have been.

Jose (hose-AY) Spanish variant of Joseph. Substitute teachers with poor eyesight will call this child Josie.

Jovan (jo-VAHN) A musky aroma encountered often in the '70s.

Juan (wan) This name allows you to refer to the very thing you mean, "this Juan," "that Juan," "which Juan?"

Judas (JOO-dis) Helped prepare Jesus' last supper, which was sacrilicious!

Juel (jewel) A family treasure. Should protect from blunt-force trauma at all cost.

Juhu (JOO-hoo) A delicious chocolate drink. Also, a greeting popular with Spanish men choosing alternative lifestyles.

Justin (JUST-in) A precursor to headline news teasers, e.g., "This Justin. What you're doing right now could cause death. . . . Story at eleven . . ."

Kash (cash) The man in black. Prone to hiding valuables.

Kay C (KAY-see) One with a bright backup band. The man

behind such smash hits as "Shake, Shake, Shake" and "I'm Your Boogeyman."

Kenneth (KEN-eth) Creepy professor with puffy hands that can't resist the feel of young nubile flesh.

Kenyon (KEN-yun) A chasm between mountains that often houses deer, scrub oak, and rattlesnakes.

Koalby (COAL-bee) The cuddly hybrid marsupial created by mating a koala and a wallaby. Hops very slowly. Also, the Texan with good teeth.

Kouvasier (koo-VASS-ee-ay) A derivative of Courvoisier, a liquor popular with the ghetto fabulous.

Kurt (curt) Child will speak only in short, rude sentence fragments. Will never let you speak.

Laddie (LAD-ee) Lassie littermate who was much less adept at going for help.

LaDell (la-DELL) LaFarmer in LaDell. LaFarmer in LaDell. Hi ho the dairy-o—LaFarmer in LaDell.

LaMond (la-MAHND) A bicycling superhero. A child with this name will be riding a two-wheeler before he can walk.

Lancer (LAN-sir) One who uses a sharp stick or an instrument to puncture boils.

Landon (LAN-duhn) One whose life of good will reach from the dirt roads of the prairie to the highways of heaven.

Laslo (LAZ-lo) High-end line of skin care products used to firm and tighten.

Lavenard (LAV-uh-nard) Famous for the purple hue of his testicles. Possible careers include circus freak and porn star.

LaZello (LA-zeh-low) A spicy Italian gelatin dessert made famous by a New Orleans chef. Bam!

Leviathan (luh-VYE-uh-than) A giant sea monster. Exception to the rule: if you hope for a child doomed to become so morbidly obese that he will have to be removed from his trailer by a crane.

LeVoid (luh-VOID) The process your French saleswoman must follow when she makes a mistake ringing you up. The ideal location to dispose of French citizens whom you have murdered in space.

Linton (LINN-tun) An often multicolored bit of fluff found in the navel. This child will feel extraneous and unwanted.

Logan (LOW-gun) The substance emitted from one's mouth after extensive throat clearing.

Lon (lahn) One who mows carpet, usually outdoors. Referred to as someone who can be walked all over.

Lord (lord) Those with strong religious beliefs will never be able to praise the child for good behavior.

Lucky (LUCK-ee) Name will be an ironic reminder of all of his failures.

Luis (loo-EECE) Most likely a busboy.

Luke (lewk) Not quite hot, not quite cold. A very average child.

Mack (mac) Generic name that bartenders use for a Pall Mall–smoking, beer-guzzling customer. Note the *k* is silent. Also, a large five-ton semi.

Major (MAY-juhr) A really big recording company. An officer in the armed forces, but not high enough on the totem pole to qualify as a namesake.

Marcus (MARK-us) Request made by female fans of famous tattoo artists during *MTV Spring Break* in Florida. Exception to the rule: last name, Oreallyus.

MarVel (MAR-vuhl) Having run out of ideas for superheros, a comic book company decides to create a superhero in its own image.

Mason (MAY-sun) A glass receptacle used for canning. Also, a bricklayer extraordinaire.

Matthew/Matt (MATH-ewe)/(mat) A dull child. Also, a piece of fabric used in front of a door for wiping one's shoes.

Maverick (MAV-rick) A renegade. Also, an appallingly bad Western starring Mel Gibson and Jodie Foster.

Mavryck (MAV-rick) Hideous, hideous variant of Maverick, which is bad enough in and of itself.

Max (maks) The top. The most. This child will be teased with a feminine napkin nickname, or mimicked with a surfer/valley girl (à la Moon Zappa) accent. This

---

The Most Unpopular Names of the 1980s

As these names were likely established by former long-haired hippies made over into cocaine-snorting yuppies with haircuts that made them look like seagulls, you would be wise to consider avoiding them as well.

Boys
Rey
Eddy
Demetris
Coby
Cade
Bruno
Travon
Taurean
Tad
Russel

Girls
Valeria
Shanice
Racquel
Quiana
Porsha
Marcela
Malia
Loni
Krystina
Kirstin

Source: Social Security Administration

child will also likely wear glasses with thick black frames and a plaid sport coat to play the ponies.

Maxwell (MAKS-well) A pseudointellectual coffeehouse regular who stirs his latte with a hammer.

Maynard (MAY-nard) A failed condiment consisting of mayonnaise, ox testicle, and mustard.

Merlin (MER-lun) A mythical wizard of great prowess but unfortunate naming.

Migdol (MIG-doll) An analgesic that relieves menstrual cramps.

Milo (My-LO) Southern expression of surprise.

Monroe (mon-ROW *or* MON-row) An unpopular and experimental hors d'oeuvre made from caviar. Also, a man of questionable sexuality living on TV in San Francisco in the '80s (his questionable sexuality is only questionable because the network at the time would not allow for clarity).

Montee (MON-tee) An icy cold dessert treat.

Nad (nad) A testicle, e.g., "I fell off my bike and cracked my Nad!"

Narcissus (nar-SISS-us) In Greek mythology a young man who was so beautiful that he was pursued by men and women. He did not return their affections and was cursed to spend his days staring at himself in a pond, where he fell in love with himself. Because the face in the pond could not love him back, Narcissus turned into a flower, wasted away, and died. But enough about me, what do *you* think of me?

Neon (NEE-on) Bright artificial light hated by all those subjected to its unflattering glow.

Nero (NEAR-oh) Though small in stature, will grow up to own a successful chain of pizza parlors. Will also have an unexplainable attachment to stringed instruments and fire.

Nestor (NES-ter) A Greek leader in the Trojan War. His military prowess gave him great respect, but his rambling storytelling and often irrelevant advice pained his friends.

Nicholas/Nick (nik-uh-las)/(nik) Often called jolly and old, this kid will be prone to shaving cuts and tobacco addiction.

Nicodemus (nick-o-DEE-mus) Skin rash often seen as a side effect of smoking.

Nixon (NICKS-on) The thirty-seventh president of the United States. Your child will most likely be prone to surreptitious behavior, including recording your conversations and having your room searched periodically by his friends.

Noah (NO-uh) A sea captain and animal breeder.

Noah-Lot (know-a-LOT) Maybe this is better than naming a child Know-It-All. Maybe.

Octavius (oc-TAY-vee-us) Latin for the eighth born. Exception to the rule: if you're headed for number eight, we salute you. Just think of the gladiatorial-themed birthday parties you could host!

Odo (oh-D'OH) Original version of the expression of surprise best voiced by Homer Simpson.

Odysseus (oh-DI-see-us) A Greek leader in the Trojan War, famed for his trickery. Prepare for a child who could lash himself to the bottom of a sheep to escape your clutches, or tie himself and his sailors to a mast in order to avoid the lure of the Sirens. And those are only two of the tricks up his sleeve. . . .

Omari (oh-MAR-ee) Didn't your grandmother collect this type of Japanese porcelain?

Omen (OH-men) A sign from the great beyond. Black cats and crows will flock to your child.

Orpheus (OR-fee-us) A mythological poet and a master of the lyre, who played so beautifully that objects (animate and inanimate) followed him wherever he went. Are you ready for a grunge band in the garage, complete with groupies?

Oscar (OS-car) A golden statuette coveted by members of the Hollywood community. An unpleasant, green-haired Muppet, who chooses to make his home in a trash receptacle.

Osgood (OZ-good) If you're looking to raise an NFL linebacker, this is *not* the name to choose.

Osmond (OZ-mond) Member of a talented family of Mormon performers. Your child will most likely be both a little bit "country" and a little bit "rock-'n'-roll."

Oswald (OZ-wald) A studious bookworm, remarkable for

his political activism and accuracy with a high-powered rifle.

Otto (AH-toe) If you're looking for a palindromic name, this is a good pick.

Owen (OWE-in) The one with the crooked nose. Also, child may experience a lifetime of feeling indebted to others.

p

Packer (PACK-er) One who packs meat or cheese and serves as the namesake for a football dynasty whose followers are identified by their garish green-and-yellow attire and triangular head wear.

Parker (PAR-ker) A valet. Also, a hearty boy. The one who doesn't sing.

Patrick/Pat (PAA-trick)/(pat) A sexually ambiguous child.

Peerless (PEER-less) One whose ability to make fine faucets is beyond compare.

Pentium (PEN-tee-uhm) A very fast, but occasionally unreliable processor used for completing multiple mathematic equations that generally leads to gamer's thumb.

Percival (PER-si-vuhl) A person born as dumb as a stump, whose childlike innocence and naïveté will somehow allow him to stumble into a position of great responsibility.

Peter (PEE-ter) Another phallic name. Also, one with severe marital problems and an obsession for pumpkin-flavored foods.

Pharaoh (FAIR-oh) An ancient Egyptian ruler prone to draining the checking account to buy excessive jewelry and wrapping the household pets in toilet paper.

Philander (fi-LAN-der) Greek lover of mankind. A command to cheat on one's spouse or significant other.

Philbert (FIL-bert) A hard nut to crack, but tasty on casseroles.

Phillip (FILL-up) The swirl of whipped cream topping on a hot fudge sundae. Will get a giggle anytime the phrase "fill up" is used.

Pierre (pee-YAIR) A beret-wearing frog with a disagreeable demeanor.

Pleather (PLEH-thur) Inexpensive, nonbreathable material often used for hooker ensembles. See also Vinyl.

Polo (POE-lo) The appropriate response to the call "Marco" when assisting a visually impaired swimmer.

Prince (printz) A nobleman who aspires to be king but will most likely see all of his foibles printed for the whole world to see in newspapers best known for their coverage of UFOs.

Pucci (POOCH-ee) Italian designer of fabulous, mod-style prints. A common nickname for dogs of mixed breeding.

Racer (RAY-sir) One who takes part in a race. While the "winner" will definitely be a "Racer," most "Racers" will be "losers."

Raekwon (WRECK-one) You will never want to lend this child your car.

Raider (RAY-dur) A well-dressed villain

whose designs on the ancient treasure will surely be foiled by our fedora-wearing hero.

Ralph (ralf) To vomit, e.g., "Are you going to Ralph?"

Rameses (RAM-seez) An Egyptian pharaoh with an absolute sense of self-importance. Also, a fine brand of condoms, often ribbed.

Ramon (ruh-MOAN) Delicious, inexpensive Chinese noodles that are easily prepared by adding boiling water. Popular with those pursuing a college education.

Randall/Randy (RAN-dull)/(RAN-dee) The kid who couldn't take his hand off his privates. Likely to become the unpopular guy at the bar. Perpetually horny.

Rebel (REH-bull) Nonconforming and fond of the color gray. Given to loud vocal expression.

Red (red) A godless communist who hates everything you stand for as an American.

Regent (REE-junt) Someone who governs in someone else's stead. Also, a morning talk show host—the one who's only slightly less annoying than his ex-cohost.

Rémy (RAY-mee) This kid is likely to end up wearing an old raincoat and living on a park bench thanks to his inordinate fondness for inebriating spirits.

Reuben (ROO-ben) A greasy sandwich made of corned beef, sauerkraut, and Swiss cheese. Serve warm.

Rex (recks) A great name for a Labrador or golden retriever.

Rhett (rett) A dashing Charlestonian who offers Scarlett O'Hara fifty dollars in gold for the pleasure of a dance.

Ricardo (ri-CAR-doh) A wealthy island owner who toyed with the lives of others and dabbled in the supernatural. Especially enjoyed entertaining small people. See also God.

Richard/Dick (RIH-chard)/(dick) Should never be used if your surname is Long, Harden, Wipe, Wad, or Less.

River (RI-vur) A talented young actor with a taste for the illicit, destined to flame out at an early age. Name should be avoided if you live in Arizona.

Robert/Bob (RAH-burt)/(bob) Fat aunts will suggest he be a UK policeman every Halloween. Also, the butt of jokes about the armless, legless man who attempts to water-ski.

Rodney/Rod (RAHD-nee)/(rahd) Another pitifully phallic name reminiscent of the Washington Monument. Jokes will be merciless.

Romaine (ro-MAYNE) A type of oddly shaped lettuce popular with washed-up sitcom actors.

Romer (ROAM-ur) An explorer who wanders aimlessly.

Romulus (ROM-you-luss) An Italian orphan given to suckling outside his species, sibling-on-sibling violence, and founding European capital cities. Also, a planetary cousin of the Vulcans. You really do need help.

Ronald (RAH-nuld) A man with big feet, high cholesterol, and a red nose; often mistaken for a lush or a short, hairy porn star.

Roscoe (ROS-coe) A sheriff's deputy in a small Southern town who exhibits an annoying laugh and poor driving skills. Enjoys the company of a hound dog and looks forward to the day when "those Duke boys get what's coming to them."

Rufus (ROO-fuss) A likely winner in the Sporting category at the Westminster Dog Show.

Ruger (ROO-gher) A German handgun popular with Japanese members of the monocle-wearing set.

Rush (rush) The act of hurrying to secure illegal prescription drugs or delivering a diatribe on any number of conservative issues.

Ryan (RYE-an) A name shared by an army private saved by Tom Hanks in 1998 and an orgasm-faking actress.

Ryder (RYE-der) A boxlike truck most often used to carry explosives and illegal aliens.

Sailor (SAY-ler) Someone looking for a good time, e.g., "Hey, Sailor, you looking for a date?"

Samuel/Sam (SAM-ewe-uhl)/(sam) A picky eater who is especially averse to eggs with a grasslike hue, and pork. He will not do anything you ask him to do. Not on a plane, not on a train. Not in a house and not with a mouse.

Scout (skowt) A boy who enjoys wearing only blue shirts covered in patches. Exception to the rule: if you happen to be naming a puppy before giving birth to your child.

Sean (seen) In middle-American English, past tense of the verb *see.*

Sebastian (suh-BAS-tyun) A bastard.

Serge (surge *or* sairge) A sudden burst of electricity.

Seymour (SEE-more) Will have a great affection for a large, flesh-eating plant. Should never be used with the surnames Butts, Porn, or Ofmyass.

Sham (sham) A fake. Sure, it's biblical, but that doesn't make it right.

Shamaine (shuh-MAYNE) A roll of toilet paper developed in the '70s that one *could* squeeze.

Shane (shane) A feeling of guilt.

Ski (skee) One of a pair of sharp, pointy planks used to travel downhill rapidly on snow. This name should be avoided by those individuals looking to join the legislative arm of the government.

Slaughter (SLAW-ter) Even if it's a family name, don't. Exception to the rule: if you're grooming your boy for a career as a professional wrestler.

Slider (SLY-der) A ruler used for making complex calculations. As a general rule, words that can also sort of be verbs do not make for healthy, esteem-producing names.

Smoky (SMOW-kee) Derogatory term for police officer. Conjures up images of classic '70s Burt Reynolds movies.

Socrates (SOCK-ra-teaze) If you're a fan of *Bill & Ted's Excellent Adventure,* this is pronounced "SO-crates."

Spencer (SPEN-sir) One who is for hire, generally. May be doomed to a lifetime as an assistant.

Starbuck (STAR-buck) Look for one on every corner, and prepare your son for a lifetime of "I'll have a tall, double no-fat cappuccino" orders. Exception to the rule: excellent opportunity for brand-name marketing deals.

Starsky (STAR-skee) Cool '70s cop played by David Soul. Or wait, was he Hutch? Who knows? Who cares? See also Hutch.

Sterile (STEHR-ill) Come on, that's just mean.

Stirling (STIR-ling) Ancient Scottish family and castle. Also, the family silver.

Stone (stown) A piece of rock. This child will be known for his cold, abrasive demeanor.

Stoney (STOW-nee) To be under the influence of an illegal herbal supplement. Child will be cursed with glassy eyes and constant hunger, but may be very popular in high school and college.

Symmion (SIM-ee-on) A child with opposable thumbs and the abilities to hang upside down and eat pounds of bananas.

Tag (tahg) German for "day." The appropriate way to praise your child with this name for good behavior is "Guten, Tag!"

Talon (TAL-un) The sharp, pointed claw on a bird of prey's foot used to capture and kill hapless rodents. Also, a short-lived, American-made, poor man's sports car.

Tanner (TAN-er) One who skins and cures the hides of animals while in the sun, without wearing sunscreen.

Tat (tat) Short form of "tattoo," a type of permanent ink decoration applied to the skin, most often adopted while intoxicated and then regretted for the rest of one's life.

Taz (taz) A cartoon devil that whirls around, wreaking havoc.

Te'quandris (tuh-KWAN-dris) Early cousin of a popular Mexican alcohol that was quickly phased out after makers realized that it just confused consumers.

Teter (TEE-ter) A tendency to wobble. Also, half a piece of playground equipment.

Thor (thor) Norse god of thunder. Also, a blond, dress-wearing superhero who fought the forces of evil with a hammer.

Thurston (THUR-sten) Island-dwelling husband of Lovey who continued to wear his pith helmet and ascot episode after episode.

Tiki Lou (tee-kee-LEW) A portly, poorly kept gentleman who runs the local Hawaiian-themed bar.

Titus (TIE-tuss *or* TITE-ass) A Roman senator and protagonist of a Shakespearean tragedy. Also, an uptight, annoying little prig.

Toah (TOE-uh) Oah Noah, I think I broke my toah!

Travis (TRAA-viss) A country singer destined to make a couple of bucks singing about his life in the trailer park.

Trey (tray) Middle English "three." Cursed with a third nipple, making junior high gym class excruciating.

Trezor (TRAY-zor) Major advance in shaving technology utilizing three blades.

Trilogy (TRIH-low-gee) A group of three. Destined for performance anxiety issues.

Tristan (TRIS-tun) Cross-dressing pop diva and expert on all things Cher. Goes by Trista on Thursday nights.

Truck (truck) Slow to accelerate and hard to stop once moving.

This name is not recommended unless you know CB lingo such as "ten-four," "ten-twenty," "smoky on my tail," and "good buddy."

Tucomah (to-CUM-ahh) A premature ejaculator.

Tugdick (TUG-dick) A baseball player who will never make it past the minor leagues.

Tut (tut) Short form of Tutankhamen, king of Egypt from 1361–52 BC. Famous only because his survivors forgot where they buried him. He's our favorite honky.

Twylen (TWY-lun) B-grade country singer obsessed with losing his horse.

Tyathos (tie-ATH-ose) An artificial feta alternative sold in bulk at Costco.

Tylen (TIE-lun) The act of laying tile.

Tylier (tie-lee-AY) A French grout designer.

Tyre (tire) To grow bored or impatient. Chronically exhausted. Also, the covering of a wheel made out of rubber and filled with compressed air. A child with this name is destined to suffer from Attention Deficit Disorder and flatulence.

Tyreek (tie-REEK) A home improvement handyman who didn't shower for day two.

Udolf (YOU-dolf) Little-known German politician overshadowed alphabetically by his cousin.

Ugo (YOU-go) Small Yugoslavian motor vehicle known for being underpowered and unreliable.

Uilliam (WILL-yum) Child will be doomed to a lifetime of being confused with a certain item on the periodic table of elements.

Ukiah (you-KIE-uh) Child may be confused with a Chevrolet SUV.

Ulysses (you-LISS-eez) The hero of Homer's *Odyssey*. The given name of the most drunken president in the history of the United States.

Urban (UR-bun) One who dwells within a city or densely populated area. A true metrosexual.

Utah (YOU-tah) A state known for its pioneer spirit, radical religious beliefs, and the saltiest stagnant pond in the world.

Uzi (OO-zee) An Israeli-made submachine gun popular for its compact size. Also, to fester with puss, e.g., "This scab on my knee is all Uzi!"

Va Loy (va-LOY) A fabric hybrid with the strength of metal and the texture of velour.

Vachel (VAY-chel) A small French cow. Also, a Russian transvestite.

Valgene (VAL-gene) A fast-acting cream used to treat yeast infections.

Valiant (VAL-yent) A brave prince destined to a life of bowl cuts.

Valno (VAL-no) An industrial oil-cutting solution used in fast-food restaurant grease traps.

Van (van) A boxlike motor vehicle, the white windowless variety being the conveyance of choice for kidnappers and miscreants.

Vane (vayne) A blade attached to a shaft that is moved by fluid. The inclusion of "shaft" and "fluid" in the definition should dissuade you from this name.

Vanoy (vah-NOY) An Australian boxlike motor vehicle, e.g., "That's my Van, oy!" See also Van.

Vegas (VAY-gus) A town full of sinners and whores. Child will be plagued by the saying, "What happens in Vegas stays in Vegas."

Veikko (VEE-koe) A Finnish activist in the antiapartheid movement. Not as effective in Finland as he could have been in South Africa.

Vekvek (VEK-vek) Artificial wood used for exterior decking.

Vernal (VER-null) Utah desert area well known by fossil hunters as the home of Dino the pink dinosaur.

Verv (verv) Energetic and exciting. Destined to be a male cheerleader or Broadway dancer.

Victor (VICK-ter) Winner. Also, effective stage name for male impersonators.

Vinyl (VIE-null) A flexible, shiny faux leather used to make unattractive furniture and clothing. See also Pleather and Huggy Bear.

Vincent (VIN-scent) That great scary voice from the haunted house at Disneyland.

Viper (VIE-per) A poisonous, legless, belly-crawling reptile with bad eyesight, whose only purpose in life is to eat rodents and procreate.

Vladimir (VLAH-duh-meer) A fifteenth-century Slavic ruler known for impaling and brutally torturing thousands of his subjects. He is also widely believed to have been a blood-sucking ghoul.

Wade (wade) To walk in or through water, from the Old English for "river crossing." Isn't afraid to wear capri pants.

Wagner (WAG-on-her) Maker of fine power tools and paint sprayers.

Waldo (WALL-doe) A bespectacled, wool-hat-and-striped-shirt-wearing character. A child with this name will be driven insane with taunts of "Where's Waldo?" Known to often wander off.

Walker (WAH-ker) A Texas law enforcement officer (played most convincingly by Chuck Norris). A child with this name will feel compelled to wear ten-gallon hats and enormous belt buckles. Also may be drawn to the martial arts.

Wayne (wane) To gradually decrease or deflate, as in, "My interest in him is Wayneing."

Wex (wecks) A New Age exercise for developing biceps and triceps: Wex on, Wex off.

Wilber (WILL-burr) A talking pig with an affinity for spiders.

William/Willie (WILL-yum)/(WILL-ee) Also known as Slick, a child with this name will not be able to duck comparisons to the forty-second president of the United States or an angry, animated, Scottish groundskeeper. Later in life women will say this name with a questioning upward lilt and a wink.

Wisely (WIZE-lee) With wisdom. You might as well name your son Teacher's Pet, considering how the kids at school will react every time the teacher says his name.

Wolfe (wulf) A carnivorous mammal related to the dog. As a teen, a boy with this name will only feel comfortable dating in groups. Later in life he will be drawn to seedy nightclubs.

Wolfgang (WULF-gang) A somewhat effeminate chef, and a composer with a creepy German accent.

Woodrow (WOOD-row) British slang for an erection. Avoid any names with "wood."

Woody (WOOD-ee) While marvelous in one-on-one encounters, embarrassing in most group situations. Also, a small red bird that pecks on trees and has an annoying laugh. British slang for an erection.

Worley (WERE-lee) An Old English name meaning "an erection." A pubescent rite of passage where a nerd's head is placed in a toilet and repeatedly flushed, giving his hair a swirled appearance.

Wouter (WOW-tur) An electric woodworking tool. Also a Sears hardware department manager recognized for top sales in wenches and skwew dwivews.

Wright (right) Correct. Mr. Wrong.

Wyatt (WHY-it) A member of Wild West law enforcement remembered for a shooting incident at the OK Corral. Will have difficulty obtaining a concealed weapons permit.

Wyclef (WHY-klef) A Y-shaped facial deformity generally found around the eyes. Often corrected by surgery, this defect encourages men to grow unibrows.

Wylie (WHY-lee) A haggard coyote. This child will have remarkable drive, yet be prone to failure. Also, good with kits.

Popular Names in Hungary

Aside from Goulash and Ferenc Rahozzi, Hungary has introduced a slew of names for use with our children. These names all appear to be useful at first glance. But step carefully. If your child is slight, and more Aryan than Ashkenazi, a Boldizsar may backfire (see Reverse Assimilation, p. 7). These are the most popular names in Hungary and, as such, should be avoided.

Boys	Girls
Adelbert	Agoti
Arpad	Anci
Bartalan	Angyalka
Boldizsar	Bertuska
Ferenc	Borhala
Fulop	Boriska
Gabor	Czigany
Gazsi	Dorika
Gyuzsi	Emesztina
Kelemen	Evacska
Moricz	Fereng
Neci	Frici
Poldi	Gizi
Rez	Hajna
Samuka	Ibolya
Sebestyen	Janka
Tabor	Linka
Vidor	Orzsebet
	Zsa Zsa

Xing (zhing) A neutral name. From a popular Chinese surname meaning "born of woman." A punchline. The child will most likely crave cream-filled, frosted snack cakes.

Xion (ZIE-on) Underground dance club and headquarters for humanity in the future.

Yanni (YAHN-ee) Greek form of John. One who plays woodwind instruments and sports long, chemically curled hair.

Yaqui (YAH-kee) Not good. Nicknames

will include yucky, icky, and sticky. Most likely a nose picker. Also, a fine Japanese dish.

Yeager (YAY-ger) Slang for time to get drunk. Popular in bars and fraternities.

Yoder (YO-durr) The New England pronunciation for Yoda, the ancient and revered Jedi master.

Yogi (YO-gee) A person of the Yoga practice. Also, over-weight from eating too many peanut-butter-and-jelly sandwiches. Smarter than the average bear.

Yule (you'll) A gaudily decorated chunk of dead tree burned during the Christmas holiday. Families with the surnames Log or Tide should avoid this name entirely.

Z

Zachary/Zack (ZACK-uh-ree)/(zack) All variations of "wacky" will be used to describe this child. Toward puberty, it will take on a meaning other than silly.

Zann (zan) Street slang for a prescription antianxiety drug. This child will be afraid of nearly everything.

Zebediah (zehb-uh-DIE-uh) Child will be plagued by a big ego over the literal definition of his name, "God's gift," but confounded by a low self-esteem over the fact that nobody else knows what it means.

Zebulon (ZEB-you-lun) In the Bible, a son of Jacob and Leah and the forebear of one of the tribes of Israel. A planet within the fourth Centauri nebula.

Zed (zed) The sodomy-enthralled pawn shop owner from the Quentin Tarantino film *Pulp Fiction*. The child will most likely have a proclivity for choppers (as opposed to motorcycles) and is likely to associate with dirty cops.

Zeeman (zee-MAN) Uh-huh. You said, "Zeeman."

Zeke (zeek) Early English form of search, e.g., "Zeke, and you shall find."

Zelig (ZEH-lig) Depression-era man made famous for his chameleon abilities to become like those he is with. Exception to the rule: if Orwell's prophecy comes true, name away.

Zephyr (ZEH-fur) The west wind. A fart, as in, "Did you rip that Zephyr?"

Zeppelin (ZEP-lin) From the famous musicians of Led Zeppelin. A large, rigid blimp filled with hot air.

Zeus (zoose) Greek god of the heavens. Ruler and most powerful of the Olympians. A name better used for large guard dogs.

Ziggy (ZIH-gee) A bald, bulbous-headed cartoon character with self-esteem issues. A pot-smoking master of the reggae genre of music.

Zindel (ZIN-dull) A failed blend of purple grape overshadowed and beaten to market by its less Jewish cousin.

Zippie (ZIH-pee) Prone to rapid-fire flatulence. Often called a pinhead.

girls' names

Aaronica (uh-RON-ik-uh) Veronica's more masculine twin sister. Child may attend numerous rallies for numerous causes.

Aaronita (ehr-on-EET-uh) One who has undergone an effective, albeit uneccessary, "gender reassignment" surgery.

Aasta (AH-stuh) An Italian noodle dish, usually served as the first course of a meal. Also, an unpopular, fruity diet soda blended in the early '70s.

Abcde (AB-cuh-dee) A much-shortened form of Abcdefghijklmnopqrstuvwxyz (AB-cuh-def-ghi-jekle-mnop-krstuv-wrexes). Popular front-woman for a children's group headlined by a large, yellow bird with imaginary friends. Exceptions to the rule: if siblings are Fghij, Klmno, Pqrst, Uvwxy, and of course, Zee.

Abigail (AB-i-gayl) The smart-ass who won't stop telling the other kids what to do.

Acenzion (aah-SEN-see-yawn) Celebration of Christ's uplifting into heaven. Exception to the rule: if child was born on the fortieth day after Easter.

Acharius (uh-KARE-ee-us) The fiscal year's first astrological sign. Also, a vehicle used for racing, usually as a preface to Christians being eaten by lions.

Adelaise (ad-uh-LAYZ) A thick yellow French sauce often served with beef. Also, feminine form of the popular, yet boring presidential candidate Adlai Ewing Stevenson. Child, as political namesake, will be doomed to multiple failures in races of all sorts.

Adie (AD-ee) A dilemma common with readers of women's periodicals, the condition of too much advertising space in relation to editorial space, e.g., "I can't even read this month's *Cosmo,* it's just so Adie!"

Adrama (uh-DRAHM-uh) A popular daytime television format known for its poor acting and incredible plot lines. Often referred to as "my soap" or "my story."

Ae Jae (aah-JHAY) The delicious, beef-based broth that generally accompanies a French Dip sandwich.

Aelyn (AIL-un) Not feeling well, frequently sick.

Aerie (AIR-ee) Light, fluffy, void of substance, twinkie-ish. Not only will she have a unique name, but her classmates can use it to describe the contents of her skull, e.g., "Wow, it sure is Aerie between your ears."

Affinity (uh-FIN-i-tee) A natural attraction, liking, or feeling of kinship. Child may be inexplicably drawn to a life of fetishism.

Africa (AA-freak-uh) The second largest continent of the planet Earth. A child with this name, though beautiful, will be war torn, impoverished, and prone to natural disaster. She may also grow tired of men's attempts to "return to the cradle of humanity."

Agatha (AG-uh-thuh) One with an affinity for crime dramas and murder mysteries. Generally child's term papers will follow a very similar format, with recurring historical characters, and slightly varied locations.

Agnes (AG-nus) Old and wrinkly one. Along with Zelpha and Vera, a name that should not have been used after the nineteenth century.

Ahnu (ah-NEW) Sound made when one sneezes. Child may develop a religious complex as a result of frequent "bless yous" or "gesundheits" given in response to her introduction.

Aili (EYE-lee) A seasoned Italian mayonnaise often served with crudités.

Aimee (ay-ME) One who is aimed at, as with a slingshot or high-powered rifle, e.g., "Was she doing the aiming?" "No, she was the Aimee."

Popular Names in Guam, Micronesia, and the South Pacific

Granted the combined population of Guam, Micronesia, and Kinbati is less than a million people, but popular names in this region are still a difficult sell. Again, it is important to note that if you and your family stem from this region, by all means, name your child in some manner to reflect your heritage. Additionally, merchant marines and various commercial fisherman may use these names. However, these names should never be taken out of context and used cross-culturally, for obvious reasons. For clarification, the literal definitions of these names are listed here.

Boys
Aruniui—man of the sea
Babeldaob—the upper ocean
Morelik—living on the ocean side of the atoll
Napo—wave
Ngiralmau—deep end of the lagoon
Soaladaob—one who likes the sea

Girls
Abejar—right there, at the lagoon side of the atoll
Chubasca—storm at sea
Iull—swell, on the open sea
Taitasi—no sea
Tadtasi—having no sea
Tasi—sea, ocean
Tasina—her (or his) sea

Aingee (AIN-jee) An itchy skin condition causing patches of hair loss.

Airlea (air-LEE-uh) Ethereal, heavenly, not of this world. National airline of a small European country boasting the greatest linseed oil reserves in the world.

Alabama (al-uh-BAM-uh) A state whose name is derived from the Choctaw words meaning "plant picker" and is best known as the birthplace of the Confederate Constitution. Primary crops include cotton, peanuts, and boll weevils.

Alabaster (AL-uh-bast-ur) Pasty-white daughter who will most likely burst into flames when exposed, unprotected, to the light of the sun.

Alafair (al-uh-FAIR) A country gathering featuring vegetable grow-ing contests, pie-eating contests, and if you're lucky, the world's largest pig, held in the state of Alabama. See also Alabama.

Alaska (uh-LAS-cuh) The "Last Frontier" was purchased from Russia in 1867 for far too much money and our country still hasn't found a good use for this moose-and-polar-bear-infested wasteland. Nice work, Secretary of State William H. Seward.

Albreda (al-BREED-uh) A brood mare.

Alchemy (AL-keh-mee) The miraculous power of transmuting something common into something precious. Most likely to become a black widow grifter, marrying and murdering men of means.

Aleece (uh-LEECE) A chain or strap of material on the end of which one fastens a dog.

Aleena (uh-LEEN-uh) A type of iron ore. Also a line of frozen low-calorie dinners.

Aleris (uh-LER-iss) A midsized sedan imported from Korea and given a whimsical name in a failed attempt to appeal to American car buyers.

Alexis (uh-LEX-iss) Bitchy ex-wife of Colorado oil millionaire who frequently mud wrestles with Linda Evans in a pond. Also, a luxury sedan known for its high price but smooth ride. Exception to the rule: if you live in Times Square and want your daughter to stay close . . . especially on the streets.

Aloha (uh-LOW-ha) A traditional Hawaiian greeting or farewell. Child may never know if she's coming or going.

Alondra (uh-LAWN-druh) The college dorm next to Faisan and Naranja.

Alorra (ul-ORE-uh) A small European nation nestled in the Pyrenees, whose main source of revenue is the printing of postage stamps.

Alreta (al-REE-tuh) A convenient, soy-based pocket sandwich introduced during the Atkins craze.

Alta (AL-tuh *or* ALL-tuh) A ski resort in the Wasatch mountain range of Utah known for its unpleasant attitude toward snowboarders.

Althea (al-THEE-uh) Vanessa Huxtable's troubled friend and confidante who dared to smoke in the house of famed comedian turned ob-gyn William Cosby.

Alva (AL-vuh) The beer-thirsty pronunciation for the beginning of the statement "I would like another."

Amber (AM-burr) A yellowish brown stone made from the fossilized sap of trees. Strange prehistoric insects can often be found entombed within Amber, then later made into jewelry.

Ambrosia (am-BRO-zhah) The food of the gods in ancient Greek and Roman mythology. Also, a delicious summertime dessert made from citrus slices and freshly shaved coconut. The jokes referring to "eating Ambrosia" should be enough to deter any responsible mother and father from this name.

America (uh-MAIR-i-kuh) Land of the free. Home of the brave. Not a good name for a female child if she ever plans on backpacking across Europe. Also, if she's short, kids will call her South America. If she's tall, North America. Central America will become the destination of choice for the boys.

Amity (AM-it-ee) An international, multilevel marketing organization that promotes peaceful relations and friendship. This name has also been forever tainted by a 1979 horror film starring James Brolin.

Amnesty (AM-nes-tee) Let's just hope your child never develops plans for international travel. She will, most likely, dedicate her life to the protection of human rights worldwide.

Amulet (AM-you-let) A female child with this name will date only members of the local Dungeons & Dragons circle and may, if she's lucky and skilled enough to slay the Beholder, even rise to the level of Dungeon Master! Or so they say.

Anaya (uh-NAY-uh) An exceptionally attractive country music drag performer with a signature twang in his/her voice.

Andoorie (AND-oo-ree) Sister to Ikka Masala.

Andromeda (an-DROM-eh-duh) Ethiopian princess saved from a sea monster by Perseus. While she'll most likely be at the Star Trek convention, this name, referring to the major galaxy closest to our own, will ensure lifelong geek status.

Anelle (uh-NEL) A small, pointed metal spike used in construction to hold materials together, e.g., "I hammered Anelle through that board to hold up the wall."

Angelica (an-JEL-ick) Like many names destined to become ironic, like this one will blow up in your face. Any adolescent female is bound to revolt against the unbelievably high behavioral expectations associated with this moniker and will most likely amount to nothing more than an unwed crack mother turning tricks to pay the rent on her double-wide.

Angelina (ann-juh-LEEN-uh) Full-lipped, well-bodied action heroine who is often the stuff of young men's fantasies.

Anna (ANN-uh or AH-nuh) If the first pronunciation, the nice girl next door. If the second pronnciation, the bitchy girl who lives in the vegan co-op and wears long floaty skirts with thick socks and sandals.

Anndee (ANN-dee) The unattractive, red-haired life partner of Raggedy Ann. All this time you thought the short-cropped hair and overalls meant she was a boy?

Annekette (AN-uh-ket) The art of behaving badly. Antonym: etiquette.

Apathy (AP-uh-thee) A generalized sense of carelessness or malaise. Clear a spot on your couch 'cause that's where this good-for-nothing freeloader is going to spend the next thirty to forty years listening to speed metal and playing with her piercings. Her lack of interest and passion for anything other than rotting her teeth and widening her posterior will serve you right.

Aphrodite (aa-fro-DIE-tee) Greek goddess of love and beauty similar to the Roman Venus. She'll marry a furnace repairman, but will always love a military man.

Apple (AA-pull) Shiny, red cherub of a fruit born into a family of performers. Destined for mockery, greatness, or frequent worm infestation.

Aprella (uh-PRELL-uh) Month that follows Amarcha and precedes Amaya.

Aqua (ACK-wa) A light greenish blue color that looks nice on eyelids.

Aquanetta (ack-wa-NET-uh) A '40s B-movie actress whose film credits include *Captive Wild Woman, Jungle Woman,* and *Tarzan and the Leopard Woman.* Also, a hairspray for those ladies who need "serious hold."

Aquavette (ah-kwuh-VET) A water sport diva.

Arabia (uh-RAY-bee-uh) A peninsula between the Red Sea and the Persian Gulf. Home to vast oil fields and the world's largest dairy farm.

Ariana (ah-ree-AH-nuh) A pale girl with a Confederate flag for a bedspread.

Arizoni (AIR-iz-OWN-ee) Along with Californi and Nevadi, states that Appalachian hillbillies aspire to pack up their trucks and move to.

Ashley (ASH-lee) The pretty Judd.

Asia (AY-zhuh) The world's largest continent. Also, the culinary elements responsible for the flavor in fusion foods.

Aspire (ass-PYRE) To have great ambition; to soar. A burning funeral platform reserved for jerks. Just stay away from the "ass" names. Please.

Astrolena (ass-trow-LEEN-uh) The mascot for a Texas baseball team resembling a bloated, green-and-purple Muppet. Also, a woman with a 900 number who charges $24.99 per minute to predict the future.

Atlanta (at-LAN-tuh) Notoriously hard-to-get princess in Greek mythology. The largest city in Georgia. Where the players play. Often referred to as "Hotlanta" for its humid climate and high percentage of "booty shakers."

Aubren (AWE-bren) A warm brown hair tone coveted by medium-smart blondes.

Aura (ORE-uh) A cosmic force that surrounds people and things with psychedelic colors.

Aurora (uh-RAW-rah) Strange lights in the sky visible in the Northern Hemisphere. Considered the flatulence of the gods by early peoples.

Australia (awe-STRAYL-yuh) Either the world's largest island or its smallest continent. Originally settled as a penal colony, it is largely populated by kangaroos, sheep, and the children of criminals.

Austria (AUS-tree-uh) Once the seat of power for the Austro-Hungarian Empire, Austria received a nasty spanking during World War I and was brought along for an even nastier spanking during World War II by big brother Germany. Austria now mostly sticks to making clocks, chocolate, and California governors.

Autumn (AWE-tum) Somewhere between frigid and hot.

Avani (uh-VAHN-ee) A popular brand of bottled water from the artesian springs of Tijuana.

Avis (AY-vis) A child with this name will show a strange interest in renting automobiles. She will, most likely, start by renting skates to other school children with her friends Hertz, Budget, and National.

Aynslie (ayn-SLEE) A really classy name smacking of McMansions and child beauty pageants.

Baby (BAY-bee) A young, Jewish girl post-bat mitzvah, well on her way to becoming a woman in the Catskills. She will be loved by many, but only give her heart to seemingly no-goodnik dance instructors with misunderstood pasts. Child may also tend to sleep in the middle of a room, because no one puts Baby in a corner.

Babylon (BAA-bi-lahn) The capital of ancient Babylonia, known for its great luxury and sensuality as well as vice and corruption. A female child with this name should be prepared for many jokes about her "Hanging Gardens."

Famous Plumbers

Not everyone wants his or her child to grow up to be a plumber. However, for those who want to instill a strong work ethic in their children, time spent plumbing can provide a sound education. But step carefully. Naming your child to give him or her the best shot at becoming a plumber can be dangerous. Not every Thomas Crapper has overcome his curse and gone on to greatness. A few historical plumbers have overcome their given names and become famous for something other than their skills with a two-inch pipe wrench. Remember, the names below are exceptions to the rule and should be treated as such.

Ozzy Osbourne—Prior to a brief stint in prison and a long career as a musician, Ozzy began his teenage years as a plumber.

Simone DeCavalcante (aka Sam the Plumber)—Prior to a three-year stint in prison and finally retiring in Florida, Sam began his career as a plumbing supplier for several well-known Italian-American families.

G. Gordon Liddy—Prior to a five-year stint in prison and a successful career as a radio talk show host, G built his career as an FBI "plumber" cleaning out filing cabinets of opposing political parties.

Abdul Rashid Dostum—Prior to a brief stint as the general of the Afghan puppet army run by the Soviet Union in the late 1980s, Rashid spent his time drinking whiskey and plumbing (possibly at the same time).

Joe Cocker—Prior to a successful career in the music industry, Joe got by with a little help from his friends the gas pipe wrench and yellow Teflon.

Allan Williams—Prior to a successful career managing an unknown group of no-goodnik musicians from Liverpool in 1960, Allan plumbed effectively.

Lee Marvin—Prior to shooting Liberty Valance, Lee worked as a plumber's apprentice in New York.

Gabriel Byrne—Amidst a career as a cook, a teacher, a bullfighter, a toy factory employee, and a film star, Gabriel attempted to plumb his way through Ireland.

Baltimore (BALL-tih-more) Home of such lackluster, bird-monikered professional sports teams as the Orioles and Ravens.

Bambi (BAM-bee) The poor deer whose mother was gunned down in cold blood by the heartless hunter and left as an orphan to fend for himself in the wilderness. Also, effective alter ego of many an off-off-Broadway "dancer."

Barbeli (BAR-bell-ee) An endomorph with an impressive ability to quickly down a case of Natty Light. Also enjoys doing keg stands.

Bathsheba (bath-SHE-buh) Will have a penchant for bathing in public places and arousing the lustful glances of much older men.

Beach (beech) A less than pleasant woman; also, a female dog. The jokes about crabs may, alone, be enough to make your child hate you forever.

Beefea (BEEF-ee) It's what's for dinner. With fiddle music ringing in her ears and constant calls of "Where's the Beefea?" your child will surely beg you to change her name by the time she reaches the second grade.

Belladonna (bell-uh-DON-uh) Italian for beautiful woman; also, the highly poisonous derivative of the nightshade family.

Bertha (BURR-thuh) Usually used to refer to something enormously large and ponderous, Big Bertha will undoubtedly become the other children's playground taunt of choice.

Bet'C (BET-see) The preferred vanity plate spelling for an otherwise traditional name.

Bianca (bee-AHNG-cuh) Feminine form of spray-on breath freshener popular in the early '80s.

Bijou (BEE-zhoo) A famous theater. A scion of rock royalty.

Bimberly (BIM-bur-lee) Shortened name for Kimberly, the famous bimbo. Slated to be launched as Barbie's sister in 1999, lo, a scandal involving Ben and his life partner, Ken, quashed the dream.

Bindy (BIN-dee) Both dog and daughter of the famed alligator hunter.

Birch (burch) A socially accepted substitute for "bitch" used by born-again Christians.

Blanche (blanch) To dip in hot water for the purpose of removing the skin. A child with this name will most likely graduate from torturing animals to the status of mass murderer before she is done with junior high school.

Blasé (blah-ZAY) A jaded, bored girl destined to smoke French cigarettes and wear berets.

Blenda (BLEN-duh) A kitchen appliance used by the residents of New England to whip up fruity, tropical drinks, e.g., "Ay,

Janice, mix up a coupla more a dem piña coladas in dah Blenda!"

Blessing (BLESS-ing) She won't seem like much of a blessing at 3:00 AM when you're dealing with hysterical crying, projectile vomiting, and yellow blowout diarrhea. And the child might not sleep through the night either.

Blonda (BLON-duh) Having lighter hair than the other girls, e.g., "Is she the dishwater blonde?" "No, she's the Blonda of the two."

Bonquisha (bon-KEESH-uh) A delicious breakfast food and sister of Laquisha.

Breezy (BREEZ-ee) Beautiful and relaxed, she's also going to be easy.

Brella (BRELL-uh) Short for umbrella, it will be bad luck to open her inside the house.

Brendy (BREN-dee) Screwtop brandy—all of the alcohol, none of the class!

Briana (bree-AH-nuh) A soft French cheese adored by snobs.

Bridie (BRY-dee) Wedding plans are locked and loaded. Now she just needs to find a man.

Brinderella (brin-dur-EL-uh) The little-known twin sister of

Cinderella who wasn't fortunate enough to have lost her glass slipper and was forced to continue a life of servitude.

Brittany (BRIT-nee) Commitment-phobic hillbilly with good dance moves. A small, timid dog of the spaniel variety.

Brooke (brook) A small, bubbling girl who used to frequent tennis circles.

Brunette (broon-ET) In this day of cheap and effective hair coloring, why would you limit your child's ability to explore other options? After all, blondes do have more fun.

Brunhilda (broon-HILL-duh) A large European esthetician who needs a wax more than any of her clients.

Bunny (BUH-nee) A small rodent known for its propensity to copulate frequently and give birth to a slew of offspring with little concern for their standard of living. Do you really want to be a grandparent when your child is still a preteen?

Butterfly (BUH-ter-fly) An insect with a slender body and four broad, usually colorful wings. Most commonly used as a nom de guerre for adult entertainers. See also Velvet and Cinnamon.

Cachay (cash-AY) Popular '70s eau de toilette packaged in a convenient purse pot.

Capucine (CAP-oo-cheen) An exceptionally smart breed of monkey most often seen chained to the side of a concertina begging for spare change.

Caroline (KEHR-oh-line) A door-to-door singer often seen during the holiday season.

Cashmere (CASH-meer) A prize ho, very soft, but difficult to keep clean.

Cassidy (CASS-i-dee) A single-parent family of '70s pop idols with great hair, artificially enhanced voices, and a cool bus. Also, half of a great Western.

Chalmers (CHAL-merz) Superintendent of the Springfield School District. Will tend to be verbally abusive to her underlings.

Chanel (shuh-NEL) Along with Courvoisier, Gucci, and Lexus, a popular name among (and only among!) the ghetto fabulous.

Famous Sidekicks

Every parent wants the world for his or her child, but some settle for a child destined to be second best. Many sidekicks have done rather well for themselves; however, their success is entirely dependent upon the life span of their employer. Avoid the following names of sidekicks, as such.

Ed McMahon
Robin
Cato
Tonto
Harpo
Chico
And the Other One
Minute Mouse
Ed Norton
Gracie Allen
Sancho Panza
Art Garfunkel

Chardonnay (shar-dun-AY) Her bouquet hints of green pastures, with top notes of butter, chrysanthemums, and honey, with a palate of oak on the finish. Generally best served cold.

Charissa (char-EE-za) A spicy Spanish sausage with meat of unknown origin.

Chastity (CHAA-stuh-tee) Virtuous character. Celibacy. A poor girl with this name will be destined to become the town tramp.

Cherel (sher-EL) A type of rare mushroom used in fine patés.

Cherish (CHAIR-ish) It's like a sofa, but it's not; it's like a loveseat, but it's not. It's more valued, more chair-ish!

Cherry (CHEH-ree) Peewee's favorite place to sit. The fruit of a deflowering.

Cheyenne (shy-ANN) A city in Wyoming, a nomadic Native American tribe, and a luxury sport utility vehicle.

Chinchilla Zest The outermost layer of the chinchilla, extracted with a special culinary tool, the chinchilla zester. Beware the layer just below the dermis, which can be pithy. Also, a fine but tart salad dressing.

Chloe (KLOH-ee) A name commonly used by lesbian couples for a firstborn.

Christina (kris-TEEN-uh) The one who can sing.

Cimemthymia (si-mem-THIM-ee-ah) A vicious STD cured in the early '70s.

Cinnamon (SIN-a-muhn) The dried bark of a tropical Asian tree. A popular stage name for exotic dancers. See also Velvet and Butterfly.

Cisco (SIS-ko) Will have a penchant for routers and singing about Brazilian-cut underpants.

Cleeo (KLEE-oh) Jamaican "psychic" whose infomercials bilked millions of desperate Americans out of large amounts of cash in a mass redistribution of wealth. Child may be an entrepreneur.

Cleopatra (klee-oh-PAT-ruh) Titular queen of Egypt and lover of Roman generals. Coined the phrase "what a pain in the asp!"

Cleora (klee-OAR-uh) A topical ointment used to eradicate acne.

Coco (KOH-koh) Most common name for female chimpanzees, nuts, and fashion designers. Your daughter will have hairy, prehensile toes, a rich flavor, and a flair for accessorizing.

Cola (KOH-lah) A brown, sugar-filled liquid of such high acidity that it dissolves pennies. Also, a cocaine dealer.

Constance (KON-stunse) Faithful and dependable; a child with this name will never need to rely on laxatives or fiber supplements.

Corvette (kor-VET) A type of warship, a type of American sports car, and a type of male genitalia extension.

Crescent (KRESS-unt) A cheap, canned knockoff of a famous French pastry.

Crisco (KRIS-koh) Simply put, she'll be fat in the can.

Crumpet (KRUM-pet) A spongy, English muffin–type pastry best served with tea and jam. A thrilling way to start your day!

Czarina (zar-EEN-uh) Wife of a czar or an imperial ruler in her own right. Will spend exorbitant sums of money on eggs.

Dachele (duh-SHELL) Source of processed fossil fuel, high-nitrate lunch meats, and gallon-sized carbonated beverages. "Where did you get dat hundred-eighty-ounce soda and Slim Jim snack?" "Down at Dachele."

Daffodil (DAFF-oh-dill) An early bloomer who leaves the farm to try to make it in the big city.

Daisy (DAY-zee) A desirable country cow or front-parlor maid. All the boys will ask for a dollop of Daisy. Also, child will have a penchant for old Levis, cut at the crotch, several sizes too small.

DaNae (duh-NAY) Vietnamese city known for its strategic location during the Tet Offensive.

Danetta (duh-NET-uh) The lady who sets your grandmother's hair in little metal curlers.

Danielle (dan-YELL) A bipolar rodeo queen. Do not call her Danny or fear her wrath.

D'Ann (dan) Friend of Pat, Chris, or Leslie, D'Ann will have gender identity confusion throughout her life.

Daquari (DAK-er-ee) A frozen, rum-based alcoholic beverage best served poolside.

Darnese (dar-NEESE) A method of expressing exasperation, as in "Darnese kids—they keep trampling my flower bed."

D'Asia (DAY-zhah) Didn't you already name your child this? It just sounds so familiar.

Dee-Lee (DEE-lee) Member of the male genitalia. Also, what's up or what's happeneing, e.g., "Don't touch his Dee-Lee!" Also, "What's the Dee-Lee, yo?"

Déja (DAY-zhah) I *swear* you already named a child this. Didn't you?

Delightra (duh-LYE-truh) A delicious substitute for sugar. May cause anal leakage.

Demeatrice (duh-MEET-reese) A second-rate S&M practitioner. Group discounts available.

Deputy (DEP-you-tee) Will have hangdog eyes and big ears.

Destiny (DES-ti-nee) Kismet, fate. Also, a stripper.

Divine (duh-VINE) Loveable but scary transvestite. Looked best in a housecoat.

Dixie (DICK-see) Perfect for a she-male, whether an exhibitionist or voyeur.

D'Nay (duh-NYE) To assert adamantly that something did not happen. Also, a river in Egypt.

Dodge (dahj) Children's playground game that leaves mental and/or physical scars.

Dominiqua (dum-IN-ick-uh) A small banana republic in Central America. The chief exports are coconuts, sisal, and tarantulas.

Drucilla (dru-SILL-uh) A great drag name, particularly if one is heading across the desert in a broken-down tour bus.

Eden (EE-den) The garden from which life sprang with the creation of Adam and Eve. Home also of the wily serpent who offered Eve a taste of the forbidden fruit and led to the first recorded eviction. Nice work, Eve.

Edna (ED-nuh) The great-aunt that comes to visit and takes over your room. The trade-off for the lingering old-lady smell is a crisp two-dollar bill.

Effie (EH-fee) Network censor who bleeps out all profanity for tape delay.

Elizabeth/Lizzy (ee-LIZ-ah-beth)/(LIZ-ee) An ax-wielding murderess and preteen star.

Elvira (ell-VIE-ruh) Large-breasted, Gothic late-late-night talk show host.

Emeline (EM-uh-leen) A thick, oil-based emollient used to remove mascara in the late '50s before it was discovered to have addictive properties and cause liver deterioration.

Erasmus (eh-RAZ-mus) A holiday for the eradication of stray pencil marks.

Ernestine (UR-nes-teen) Kick-ass, gum-chewing truck stop waitress who can serve the entire dinner shift without cracking a smile or running her support hose.

Europa (you-ROPE-uh) A slow, bovine girl with pretty eyes. Also, a specialized Starbucks blend.

Evangeline (ee-VANJ-ell-ine) Bus service notable for comfy seats and in-ride sermons.

Falana (ful-AN-uh) The low-fat alternative to a Spanish custard dessert.

Fannie (FAA-nee) An old-fashioned name that speaks of maiden aunts, crocheted doilies, and, sadly enough, a big fat ass.

Fanny (FAA-nee) Just name her Butt and be done with it.

Fantasie (FAN-tuh-see) This should only be used as a stage name for exotic dancers. Period. In many states, the DMV will not print this on a driver's license.

Farrah (FAIR-uh) *The* sex symbol of the '70s whose attempts at self-preservation have virtually reached mummification levels. Females with this name have absolutely no hope of growing old gracefully.

Fatima (FAHT-ihm-uh) Though popular in the Muslim world, no female child growing up in body-conscious America should have the word "fat" in her name.

Faundaree (FOUND-uh-ree) A place where metal items are fabricated through high temperatures and constant pounding.

Fawn (fawn) A deer, a female deer. Ray, a . . . oh wait. That's all wrong.

Fawn-Dew (fawn-DOO) A delicious cheesy dish. Also, the droppings of a baby deer. Make sure to read the menu carefully.

Fawntelle (fawn-TELL) The soft spot at the top of a newborn baby's head. Should harden over by one or two years of age.

Fayme (phayme) An immortal child prone to singing and dancing on the steps of public buildings, cars, and light posts in major urban areas.

Fedora (feh-DOR-uh) A man's hat. Once the hallmark of a snappy dresser, now it's just plain poseur.

Fern (furn) An ancient plant with long stems and multiple leaves with seed pods. In harsher climates, usually found in sunrooms. The plant to which people refer when they tell someone she has the intelligence of a common houseplant.

Ferol (FEAR-all) A gasoline additive that makes engines run cleaner. Also, an animal that, while technically domesticated, exhibits antisocial tendencies and often has barely detectable ringworm.

Death Row Inmates/Serial Killers

As annoying as the name Makenzeye is, naming your child after a serial killer is twice as dangerous. Many famous serial killers of the past have fallen by the wayside and are thus less familiar to parents of the next generation. As a result—and for your child's own protection—this list of the most well-known killers and infamous murderers is provided for you to avoid, both in name and otherwise.

Erzebet Bathory—the female record holder of murders

David Berkowitz—aka Son of Sam

Albert DeSalvo—allegedly the Boston Strangler

Ted Bundy—serial killer from the western states with the most made-for-TV movies produced about his travails

Jeffrey Dahmer—preferred meat

Ed Gein—inspired elements of *The Silence of the Lambs, Psycho,* and *The Texas Chainsaw Massacre*

Earle Nelson—aka the Gorilla Man

Harold Frederick Shipman—convicted of at least fifteen murders, though allegedly responsible for nearly fifty times that many

Charles Manson—lest we forget

Jack the Ripper—A legendary serial killer in the UK

Richard Ramirez—the Night Stalker

Flavia (FLAV-ee-yuh) A tasty clam.

Fulvia (FULL-vee-uh) Once in the running with anatomy classes as the funniest name for a female body part. Of late, has been replaced by Mulva.

g

Gala (GAH-luh *or* GAY-luh) Flamboyant wife of Salvador Dali. Also, a fabulous party. An especially flavorful and crispy apple used for baking or just plain snacking.

Galaxy (GA-luck-see) A far out place in the heavens. A child named Galaxy will abbreviate her name to G. when applying for an MBA program.

Garnetta (gar-NET-uh) Only semiprecious.

Garridan (GEHR-uh-dun) A shrewish, mean old woman. We know that's actually a harridan. But it's close enough.

Gazelle (guh-ZEL) A lithe, fast animal of the African savannah often seen being torn to shreds by its quadruped predators. Inevitably this name will be shortened to Gaz.

Geddy (GED-ee) Lead singer of Rush.

Geisha (GAA-shuh) A pale, quiet, subservient child adept at shiatsu massage.

Gemia (JEM-ee-uh) Lackluster superheroine whose power of turning into jewelry proved less than useful in fighting crime.

Gentle (JEN-tul) Peaceful, calm, and placid. Let's see if you think she's gentle when she starts teething.

Geo (JEE-oh) From the Greek, meaning "earth." Will be voted most likely to be a headliner for Cirque du Soleil. Small American-made compact car that resembles a roller skate.

Gertrude (GER-trood) Hamlet's mother. A good name for a maiden aunt.

Gladys (GLAD-us) aka Happy Bum.

Glamour (GLAM-or) An excellent drag name. Not so appropriate for a kindergartener who pushes little boys and forces them to eat dirt.

Glee (glee) The misty spray that emerges from underneath your tongue at inopportune, often exciting, moments.

GlenDora (glen-DOOR-uh) Long-lost twin sister of Endora, mother-in-law from *Bewitched.*

G'ni (nee) A follower of the knights who say . . .

Godiva (ga-DIVE-uh) Chocolate-loving equestrian with a dislike for clothing and taxes.

Golda (GOAL-duh) Sister of Silvera and Coppera.

Golden (GOAL-den) A child of the retriever species. Also a flaxen-haired beauty who thinks she's soooo cooool.

Grace (grayss) The most uncoordinated girl in ballet class.

Grizelda (gri-ZEL-duh) Almost certainly the name of the evil stepmother in any fairy tale, with a hair-control problem and a taste for honey.

Guinevere (GWEN-ih-veer) A beautiful queen with commitment issues.

Gypsy (JIP-see) Stage name of the most famous stripper of the twentieth century. A thief and a horse trader.

Hana (HA-nuh) Beautiful town on the eastern coast of Maui that was destroyed by a tsunami. The best part about Hana is the road there.

Hailey (HAY-lee) A weather condition characterized by hard, frozen ice balls falling from the sky.

Hallah Lujah (HA-luh LOO-yuh) A name popular in the South. Exception to the rule: if she'll have a sibling named Amen.

Halo (HAY-low) Angelic, often left behind, video game. Also, a Southern greeting.

Hannah (HAN-uh) Truly a name for a homely girl, somehow made popular in the '90s.

Harlem (HAR-lem) Manhattan neighborhood currently subject to extreme gentrification.

Harlequin (HAR-luh-kwin) Will have an unexplainable urge to wear skintight, diamond-patterned bodysuits and pointy shoes.

The Jenny Census

Everyone who grew up in the United States in the 1970s and 1980s had a large group of friends who all had to be referred to by their last names. The reason for this "family name" distinction is that all of their first names were Jenny. Granted, in the '70s and '80s the United States was much less of a global society than it is now, so not everyone knew that everyone else was named Jenny. But now that the Jennys have grown up and are producing offspring of their own, there are far fewer new Jennys being released into society at large.

Officially, the name Jennifer takes precedence over the name Jenny. However, you should not be lulled into a false sense of security that your child's full name (i.e., Jennifer) will be used for all of her (or his, poor soul) life. The following census is proof positive that there are still far too many Jennys currently residing in the USA. For safety's sake, the name Jenny should not be resurrected until the majority of Jennys currently in existence have "moved on." Simple math suggests that with an average lifespan of eighty-five years, the name Jenny will become available again for use in late 2060.

The list below suggests (thankfully) a waning popularity in the naming of one's child Jenny and/or Jennifer. Let's keep up the good work, people!

Year	Number of Jennys/Jennifers
2002	9,344
2001	9,675
2000	10,142
1999	10,866
1998	9,207
1997	12,446
1996	12,345
1995	14,186
1994	14,911
1993	17,531
1992	19,708
1991	22,926
1990	24,661
1980–1989	465,120
1970–1979	603,720

Source: Social Security Administration

Hebe (HEE-bee) High-school nickname for many Jewish-American students living outside New York or Los Angeles.

Hedwig (HEAD-wig) Currently immortalized as a not-quite-transgendered individual.

Helga (HELL-guh) Will wear a helmet with horns and serve warriors pitchers of mead.

Heloise (HELL-o-weeze) Will annoy other children by offering unsolicited but helpful household hints such as how to deep-clean a kitchen sink with an old pair of pantyhose and white vinegar. Also, used as a greeting for asthmatics.

Henrietta (hen-ree-ET-uh) A small cat with a speech impediment and apparent domestic partner of X the Owl.

Hereditary (ha-REH-dih-teh-ree) What you name a daughter when your best friend picks your first choice, Genetic.

Hestia (HEST-ee-uh) A virtual unkown in Greek mythology. If you're going to pick a classical name, why not pick a better-known goddess?

Hilda (HILL-duh) Will keep a small flock of goats and wear lederhosen. Also, has an inoperable facial mole.

Hillary (HILL-a-ree) Some will perceive her as assertive, others simply as a bitch.

Honey (HON-ee) A sweet, sticky liquid alternative to sugar. Also, a pole dancer.

Hosana (ho-ZAN-uh) Subject of a popular pioneer song that speaks of western expansion.

Hydra (HIGH-druh) In Greek mythology a multiheaded water snake with a dog's body and the uncanny ability to regrow two heads in place of one. Have "the talk" with this one early on.

Icy (EYE-cee) Frozen slushy drink available at discount stores. Stain is impossible to remove when it falls on car seats.

Ida (EYE-duh) A common contraction. "If Ida known you were coming, Ida baked a cake."

Iman (ee-MAHN) Likely to be a famous model who married a rock star.

Imari (ih-MAR-ee) A type of Japanese porcelain.

Imogene (IH-moh-jeen) A popular entertainer who endorses denture adhesive.

Isabella (iss-uh-BELL-uh) A beautiful Italian actress whose film credits range from *Blue Velvet* to *Roger Dodger.*

Isadora (is-uh-DOOR-uh) Prone to wearing long scarves, riding in open convertibles, and interpreting complex emotions through the dance.

Isis (EYE-sis) Egyptian goddess and '70s female empowerment superheroine.

Ivaloo (EYE-vuh-loo) UK usage to explain that your house has indoor plumbing.

j

Jade (jayd) A precious green stone used to cover windows.

Jamboree (jam-bor-EE) A large scout gathering, featuring tent-pitching, campfire songs, and s'mores making. May involve singing bears.

Janet (JAN-et) Silicone-enhanced singer/dancer/songwriter prone to wardrobe malfunctions.

Jasmine (JAZZ-min) A sweet-smelling tropical flower and Disney princess.

Jemima (juh-MY-muh) Apron-wearing, kerchief-headed doyenne of breakfast foods. Often confused with her nemesis, the living syrup bottle.

Jenna (JEN-uh) A nickname for Virginia; also, a hard-drinking presidential daughter.

Jessica (JESS-i-cuh) Likely to think nobody likes her, since everyone she meets will immediately sadden as they recall the baby who fell into a well.

Jilt (jilt) Abandon a significant other without warning.

Jinx (jinks) Something or someone that causes bad luck. Will always be the other woman.

Joi (joy) Wife of famous but loudmouthed morning talk show host.

Jools (joolz) Big, fancy precious stones, as in "Get my Jools, honey; we're going out!"

Joyeux Noël (jhwah-YOU-no-well) Why, thank you! And a Happy Chanukah to you.

Jubilee (jew-bill-EE) Festive commemoration of an anniversary involving yarmulkes.

Kaprice (kuh-PREECE) A professional ice dancer who is limited to the chorus. Also, a fine but oily salad made of tomato and mozzarella.

Kassia (KASH-uh) Constellation or a breakfast cereal. Endomorph.

Kenya (KEN-ya, *or* if you're a member of the British upper class, KEEN-ya) An African coastal country with a landscape that ranges from savannah to veld. Also, a runway model.

Kepi (KAY-pee) A French military cap that can be worn at a jaunty angle. Also, an acronym for "kitchen patrol," a punishment that often involves peeling potatoes.

Kinda (KIND-uh) Something that isn't quite one thing, but also not quite another, e.g., "Hey, Mom, I'm Kinda pregnant."

Kiora (kee-OR-ah) A small crown worn by pageant contestants on an island reality show.

Krichelle (krih-SHELL) Will get louder and louder, sometimes apparently without warning.

Bart Simpson Prank Calls

Nearly everyone, at some point in his or her life, has called a random stranger on the phone to ask for a cleverly devised set of names that, when pronounced, make the receiver appear extremely foolish. But perhaps no prank caller in the past hundred years has been more effective than Bart Simpson. Both the Dick and Hunt families have been careful for generations—and will continue to be in the future. But for other, less common family names, we provide this list as a means of saving your child a lifetime of misery.

I.P. Freely
Jacques Strap
Al Coholic
Oliver Clothesoff
Seymour Butz
Homer Sexual
Mike Rotch
Hugh Jass
Bea O'Problem
Amanda Huggenkiss
Ivana Tinkle
Anita Bath
Anita Man
Maya Buttreeks
Eura Snotball
Ollie Tabooger
Heywood U. Cuddleme

Kris Miss (CHRIS-muss) A religious holiday that occurs four days after the winter solstice. The other white Chanukah.

Kylie (KHY-lee) Dr. Welby's young associate.

L

Laalaa (just like it looks!) One of the four colorful Teletubbies—we're not sure which one. Name a child this, turn on daytime TV, and you'll know soon enough.

LaBerta (la-BERT-uh) In French, the feminine for Bert. Or so her parents would like to think . . .

LaDoya (luh-DOY-uh) One of the original Jackson 6, who after sprinkling itchy powder into her brother Michael's pants, was quickly relegated to wardrobe consultant. She is currently employed by her sister, Janet.

Lady (LAY-dee) Give a girl a touch of class! No need to marry a lord—this girl's a real powerhouse in her own right. Also, a popular name for female water dogs.

LaFawnduh (la-FAWN-da) The answer an angry Frenchman might give when asked a silly question about the gender of a deer. Also, someone who might work as a political intern in the White House and engage in an extramarital affair.

Lakeesha (la-KEESH-uh) A lightly crusted egg dish that real Frenchmen don't eat.

LaPhyllis (la-PHIL-iss) A French female comedian known for her rapid-fire stand-up routines and outlandish hair.

Larissa (la-RISS-uh) Russian diminutive of Lara. Suggests a beautiful, tiny woman with big eyes who could drive a troika in a blizzard while being chased by wolves.

Latrina (la-TREEN-ah) Why not just name a daughter Toilet and be done? Concerned in-laws should call child protective services now.

Launa (la-OO-nuh) Spanish or Italian derivative for "The One." Also, the name of a pop hit by a second-generation Latin heartthrob.

Lawn (lahwn) A light cotton fabric, often dyed in pale colors. Also, that vast expanse of green (or brown) outside your window.

Lexine (lex-EEN) Material used to make the little envelopes that contain stamps in post office vending machines.

Lillian (LIL-ee-un) Your grandmother's mahjong partner.

Loki (LO-kee) Norse god of mischief or trickery. Phlegm.

Lolita (lo-LEE-tah) Variant of Lola. Also, the subject of Vladimir Nabokov's novel of obsession. Are you ready to name your sweet baby daughter after a nymphet who first evoked the phrase, "Lolita, light of my life, fire of my loins"?

Lonica (LON-ick-uh) Girl of a thousand faces. Also, an off-brand supplier of office equipment.

Lovee (LOV-ee) Though trapped on a desert island with six others, throughout the hardship she never lost her sense of privileged superiority!

Lucinda/Lucy/Lucia (loo-SIN-dah)/(LOO-sea)/(loo-CHI-ah) Will steal the football away from tenderhearted, roundheaded boys. May inspire the creation of a He-man Woman Hater's club.

Lucretia (loo-KREE-sha) The excretion of fluids caused by watching live-action remakes of classic Dr. Seuss stories.

Lulu (LOO-loo) Variant of Louisa. Also, variation of "doozy" in old '30s movies that included as their stock characters the madcap heiress and the hard-boiled newspaperman.

Luny (LOO-nee) An insane bird known for its less-than-graceful flight.

Maddeysen (MAD-ih-son) A variation on the surname of our nation's fourth president, scion of a notable Virginia family. Sometimes striving to be different is just plain wrong.

Madge (madj) A woman who frequently exclaims, "Your soaking in it!" with little additional explanation. Also, British tabloid, meaning "Madonna."

Magalita (mag-uh-LEE-tuh) Popular rum-based cocktail. Also, a miniflashlight. Also, a stiff Mexican beverage plus the worm, minus the lime.

Magdalene (MAG-duh-len) Most commonly associated with a long-haired woman of former ill repute who washed the feet of Jesus Christ. The origin for the Hollywood stock figure of the hooker with the heart of gold.

Mage (mayj) A powerful, if incredibly geeky, player of the game Dungeons & Dragons who wields the power of magic! Or so they say.

Magpie (MAG-pie) A black-and-white cowbird attracted by shiny objects and dead animals on the side of the road.

Maia (MY-ah) Greek spring goddess. Also, Italian-American possessive used by little, Italian, toddlers.

Malva (MAL-vuh) Greek, meaning "soft." Perilously close to Seinfeld's Mulva.

Marquessa (mar-KESS-a) Host island of a reality show designed to see how long contestants can be stranded on an island and forced to vote one another off the show without going insane.

Marveline (MAR-vuh-leen) Maker of fine motor oil that declared bankruptcy after failing to secure the lucrative NASCAR audience.

Marvella (mar-VELL-uh) After running out of good comic book ideas, the Marvel Comics company decided to create a heroine in its own likeness.

Mary (MAIR-ee) Gentiles only, please.

Mary Jane (mair-ee-JANE) Evokes wonderful memories of patent leather shoes, penny candies, and Pink Floyd's *Dark Side of the Moon*.

Matilda (ma-TILL-duh) A rotund Australian woman descended from hearty penal-colony stock.

Infamous Dictators

The problem with evil dictators is that they keep popping up. As a result it is difficult not to name your child after one (case in point, Adolph Coors). The best you can do is double-check the following list against your own short list and try to avoid these names as well as the names of any other political figures currently in power around the globe.

Sani Abacha, Nigeria

Idi Amin, Uganda

Chiang Kai-shek, Republic of China

Fancois Duvalier, Haiti

Francisco Franco, Spain

Mu'ammar al-Gadhafi, Libya

Adolf Hitler, Germany

Saddam Hussein, Iraq

Kim Jong Il, North Korea

Ferdinand Marcos, Philippines

Robert Mugabe, Zimbabwe

Benito Mussolini, Italy

Manuel Noriega, Panama

Augusto Pinochet, Chile

Pol Pot, Cambodia

Joseph Stalin, USSR

Suharto, Indonesia

Charles Taylor, Liberia

Josip Broz Tito, Yugoslavia

Hideki Tōjō, Japan

Mao Ze-dong, People's Republic of China

Mauvia (MAW-vee-uh) Though attractive, Mauvia always had a somewhat unhealthy hue to her complexion.

Meadow (MED-oh) A lovely, verdant field. Also, the daughter of a psychopathic but strangely endearing television mob capo.

Mecca (MEK-uh) Birthplace of Mohammed and site of annual pilgrimage made by many famous boxers.

Medhina (muh-DEE-nah) Both funky and cold.

Medusa (muh-DOO-suh) A woman so terrifyingly ugly that one look at her would turn a man to stone. Have fun listening to her cry herself to sleep after four years of high school and no boy has had the guts to ask her out.

Melga (MELL-guh) A thick, persistent phlegm that often accompanies a bronchial infection.

Mercedes (mur-SAY-deez *or* MUR-sa-deez) High-end luxury automobile or Spanish dancer.

Mia (ME-uh) A very selfish Italian girl.

Mikelle (MEEK-ell) Is it Mike? Michelle? Exception to the rule: if one of you wanted a boy and the other wanted a girl, this compromise may be the only way to save your marriage.

Mirage (mur-AZH) An optical illusion promising water in a desert. Also, a casino in Las Vegas.

Misty (MISS-tee) Foggy, cloudy, and unclear. Also, on the verge of crying, e.g., "Every time I watch *Beaches* I get all Misty."

Modesty (MOD-us-tee) Quality of being humble. Also, a feminine hygiene product.

Monica (MON-i-cah) A cigar-smoking intern made irresistible by a blue dress.

Morgan (MORE-gun) Unbelievable wife of a Saturday night character.

Morona (mor-ON-uh) Feminine form of Moron.

Mowicha (mo-WITCH-uh) A sandwich made from lawn clippings.

Nafeteria (naff-uh-TEER-ee-uh) A place where you pick out various food items set forth in a long display. Oh, wait.

Natalie (NAT-uh-lee) You take the good, you take the bad, you take them both and then you have the fattest girl at school.

Nauvoo (NAW-voo) A town in Illinois unfriendly to religious pioneers.

Nebula (NEB-you-lah) A grouping of distant stars, but also a big gassy area in the sky. Probably best avoided.

Nefertiti (nef-ur-TEE-tee) An Egyptian queen who looked hot, was bald, and married her brother.

Nevada (ne-VAD-uh, if you're a westerner, *or* ne-VAHD-uh, if you're from the East Coast) A state best known for its sagebrush, gambling, and legal prostitution!

Nike (NIE-kee *or* NEE-kay) Greek goddess of victory. Also, inevitably, a brand of running shoe, golf ball, and overpriced clothing.

Norberta (nor-BERT-uh) By putting Norbert in the feminine form, it doesn't make it better. Not at all.

Octavia (ock-TAY-vee-uh) The eighth of something. If she is your eighth child, you should stick with something simple like Jane or Ann, because you're going to forget them.

Odalisa (oh-da-LEE-suh) The ugly cousin of da Vinci's well-known subject.

Olive (AHL-uv) A savory fruit of the genus *Olea*. It is common to place your fingertips inside the black ones and to submerge the green ones in a mixture of gin and vermouth.

Olivia (oh-LIV-ee-uh) One who wants to get active, or physical, most frequently while wearing Lycra or vinyl.

Ooana (oh-ANN-uh) Surely to be shortened to Ana, the only time she will hear her full name is at the height of her partners' pleasure.

p

Pagan (PAY-gun) Lead character in the '80s romance novel *Lace* by Shirley Conran. In the movie version Phoebe Cates, as a famous, orphaned porn star, posed the famous question, "Which one of you bitches is my mother?" to Pagan and her two friends from finishing school.

Panache (pah-NASH) A sense of flamboyant style.

Panda (PAN-duh) A large, black-and-white fuzzy mammal that eats bamboo shoots and never looks at people in the zoo.

Pandora (pan-DOOR-uh) One who unleashes a pox upon the world when she loses her virginity.

Pansy (PAN-zee) As long as this name is for a daughter, fine. Never, but never, use a spring flower name for a son . . . unless it's Snapdragon and you live in Chelsea.

Paradise (PAIR-a-dice) Let's just say it. Name a child Paradise and you raise a stripper.

Paris (PEHR-iss) The capital of France that, while beautiful, festers with poor personal hygiene, ethnocentrism, and dog poo. Also, a hotel heiress known for her skills as an amateur videographer.

Parkarette (par-kar-ETTE) A tiny but strangely comfortable valet parking lot.

Passion (PASH-un) An intense emotion. Also, the signature perfume of an over-the-hill actress.

Patchouli (puh-CHEW-lee) The hideous-smelling signature perfume of the hippie.

Patsi (PAT-see) A daughter who always takes the brunt of her brothers' cruel jokes.

Peace (peece) A sense of calm. Also, a section of cake.

Peaches (PEECH-iz) Fruits, a term of endearment, another headline stripper.

Pearl (purl) A highly valued white or black gem created by the irritation of foreign matter within the shell of a mollusk.

Pebbles (PEH-bulls) Daughter of Fred and Wilma Flintstone. Also, a '70s singer best known for her hit "Do You Want To Ride in My Mercedes, Boy?"

Polly (PAHL-ee) A naive child.

Pork Chop (POKE-chop) A portion of meat cut from the flesh of a pig. Delicious when served with applesauce on Yom Kippur.

Porsche (POR-shah) A car popular with the midlife-crisis set. Expensive to procure and cost-prohibitive to maintain. Remarkable for the whiney note of its exhaust.

Portia (POR-shah) One of the satellites of Uranus.

Precious (PREH-shuss) A child so highly valued by those around her that it will lead to strife. It will not be uncommon to hear shouts of "No, I wants to hold the Precious!"

Princess (PRIN-sess) A high-maintenance child given to tea parties, tantrums, and ordering the execution of her dollies for their insolence.

Prudence (PROO-dents) A cautious Pilgrim most comfortable when clad in a bodice and floor-length skirt.

Purity (PURE-ih-tee) The state of being pure.

Pussy (PUSS-ee) Though an endearing

term for a cat, when this name is applied to a man's physical prowess, or the anatomy of a woman, it is less than endearing. This name should be avoided at all cost!

Queen (kween) A man who enjoys dressing as a woman and performing dance numbers in front of small crowds while lip-synching to songs by Cher and Abba.

Queenie (KWEEN-ee) An obese cat that has developed a taste for tuna fish and is unable to walk four steps without passing out from exhaustion.

Quorum (KWORE-um) Similar to a minion, only not as many Jews.

Rachel (RAY-chel) A hairdresser's dream client who always has a story about her crazy friends and hunky husband.

Rainbow (RAYN-bo) The proud banner of the homosexual community. That's not a pot of gold you'll find at the end!

Raine (rayn) The Christian name of the Countess Spencer, stepmother of the late Diana, Princess of Wales. Known to Her Royal Highness and her brother as Acid Raine.

Rave (rayv) A dance party held in a warehouse or field populated by strangely dressed preteens high on illicit drugs and fixated on glow-in-the-dark sticks. May lead to a life of DJ-ing.

Raven (RAY-vun) A large, black bird with an ear-splitting call that enjoys eating roadkill and stealing shiny, worthless trinkets.

Rayette (ray-ETTE) A really small piece of sunshine.

Rayna (RAY-nuh) The stuff that falls in Spaina, but mostly on the plaina.

Regan (REE-gun) A weapon used by science fiction war heros in futuristic films of the '50s, '60s, and '70s. Gave way to the more powerful Laysure in the early '80's.

Rhiannon (ree-ANN-un) Subject of that Fleetwood Mac song.

Rhodendra (ro-DEN-drah) Lacking the pleasant scent of its cousin, Rhododendron, Rhodendra was never popular with gardeners.

Rhys (rees) A type of monkey popular for use in horrific medical experimentation.

Riddle (RID-ul) A grown man who enjoys wearing brightly colored spandex bodysuits pulled up past his navel, while spouting annoying rhymes.

Riley (RYE-lee) The bespectacled center square.

Rodana (ro-DAWN-uh) Along with Mothra and Gamera, this giant flying reptile terrorized Japan for many years before being defeated by Godzilla.

Rosebud (ROZE-bud) A slightly burned Christmas sleigh.

Rumer (ROO-mur) It's not a confirmed fact; it hasn't come through official channels; it's a . . .

Sabbath (SAA-bath) The greatest heavy-metal band of all time! And that time the lead singer bit the head off a bat was really all just a big misunderstanding, you see, because he thought it wasn't real.

Sabre (SAY-burr) A long, sharp, slightly curved sword that somewhat resembles the teeth of a large cat driven into extinction by our caveman ancestors.

Sachet (sa-SHAY) The way a gay cowboy walks. Also, a scented knickknack for an undergarment drawer.

Saffron (SAFF-run) Subject and object of obsession in the '60s classic "I'm Just Mad About Saffron." Also, the world's most expensive spice, derived from the crocus flower.

Saga (SAH-gah) An interminable story involving giants and fire and mead. Just buy the Cliffs Notes.

Saige (sayj) A plant whose aroma, when in bloom, has been likened to perfume . . . deep in the heart of Texas.

Samantha (suh-MAN-tha) A name popular with transsexuals and white witches. Also, the sitcom character most likely to get an STD.

Savannah (suh-VAN-uh) A low-lying coastal Georgian city. Most people who name their daughters this have never been there.

SeaBreaze (SEE-breeze) A really bad women's perfume (but effective facial wipe) from the '80s.

Season (SEE-zun) To flavor food with grains, flakes, or seeds.

Shazzam (shuh-ZAAM!) An eight-foot-tall genie who plays center for the LA Lakers.

Shazzanna (shuh-ZAAN-uh) Younger sister and impetuous crime-fighting sidekick of Shazzam.

Shelagh (SHEE-law) Celtic word meaning "blind." With any luck she'll be a triplet, and you can name her sisters Bodhar (deaf) and Balbh (dumb), and her brother Tommy.

Shenandoah (shan-en-DOH-uh) A mighty river and the subject of the '70s musical about manifest destiny.

Sienna (see-EN-uh) The ugliest crayon.

Sierra (see-AIR-uh) Spanish for "mountain range." A child with this name will feel very in touch with the environment, choose not to shower or shave her armpits, and obsessively follow a "groovy" band around the country in a dilapidated VW van.

Skye (sky) The expanse of air covering the earth. The heavens. A child with this name will, no doubt, be as vacant and prone to wind as that region.

Skylar (SKY-lar) Fabled hostess of the mile-high club.

Sleeza (SLEEZ-uh) A sexually promiscuous female. Children with this name will be able to choose from a wide array of careers including pole dancer, masseuse, and prostitute.

Star (If you can read it, you can say it.) A luminous celestial body. A celebrity. A child with this name will be neither of these things, and will most likely end up living in a trailer park, lamenting missed chances at fame and fortune.

Stormy (STORE-mee) Affected by storms. Tempestuous. Emotionally unstable. See also Tempest.

Sugar (SHUH-ger) A powdered substance, white when pure. Unfortunately, with a name like Sugar, she won't stay pure for long.

Sumner (SUM-nehr) A fort in New Mexico where thousands of Apache and Navajo Indians were held prisoner in the 1800s. Many died. Thanks for bringing that up.

Sunny (SUH-knee) Exposed to or abounding in the death-giving rays of the sun. See also Sunshine.

Sunshine (SUN-shyn) The light from the sun. These irritating rays are known to cause cancer and severe burns. A child with this name may not cause cancer but will definitely be irritating.

Swayze (SWAY-zee) The mullet-bedecked star of films such as *Dirty Dancing* and *Roadhouse*. Though this child may meet with success early in life, a series of bad choices will cause her to disappear into oblivion while still in her prime.

Tamette (tam-ET) A pocket tambourine. Name popular with circus fans.

Tamilisia (tam-ill-EE-see-yuh) A rare form of memory loss caused by being struck in the head with a tamale.

Tandy (TAN-dee) The childish pronunciation of Candy. Thinking she is speaking baby talk, strangers will be give her no respect, and she will be laughed at during job interviews.

Taryn (TEHR-in) An inhabitant of the planet Earth. The child will only be able to develop lasting friendships with fans of *Star Trek*.

Tea (t) The dried leaves of a shrub cherished by the British when it is soaked in scalding water and consumed with small cookies in the most snotty way possible. Also, the surname of famed "boxer" who beat Rocky Balboa in the second, third, or fourth sequel.

Tempest (TEM-pissed) Furious agitation or commotion. A child with this name will find calm only after destroying every piece of household furniture you own. See also Stormy.

Tennille (ten-EEL) One half of the greatest singing duo of all time, best known for their hit single "Muskrat Love." See also Captain.

Thankful (THANK-full) Aware and appreciative of a benefit. And, believe me, the boys will be.

Tiara (tee-AHR-ah) An ornament, often jeweled, worn on the head. Not quite a crown, not quite a headband. This child will be destined for plastic surgery and pageant life.

Tonia (TOW-knee-ah) A unit of weight measurement equivalent to 2,000 US pounds. A big girl. Latin beyond praise.

Trauma (TRAW-muh) An event or situation that causes great distress and disruption. Much easier than having that "You were an accident" conversation later in life.

Treasure (TREH-zhur) Valuable or precious possessions often kept in a chest or box. A parent who gives a child this name should be prepared to guard that box carefully.

Trinity (TRIN-it-ee) A group consisting of three members. How many strippers' names can we fit into this book? Honestly, how many?

Trinket (TRING-ket) A small, trivial thing. A child with this name will have the self-worth of a gnat.

Tryst (trist) A clandestine meeting between two filthy, cheating, dishonest lovers. Wives and girlfriends will never trust a young woman with this name.

Ubah (YOU-bah) A large brass horn. This child will be a band geek, the fat one at the end who can't march on beat.

Uma (OO-ma) A tall, thin actress who leaves cheating husbands in the dust. Also, a lizard with fringed toes.

Unique (YOU-neek) The only one of its kind. Having been in the top one thousand US baby names since 1995, a child with this name will be anything but.

Urania (you-RAY-knee-uh) A troubled nation formerly a member of the Union of Soviet Socialist Republics. Located somewhere around Lithuania or Albania, or one of those places. A radioactive substance used in weapons of mass destruction. Although never officially discovered, we know it's out there.

Ursa (ER-suh) A Latin name meaning "she-bear." Prone to hair-control problems and obesity, a child with this name will never find happiness.

Ursula (ER-suh-luh) A North American butterfly, nearly black with red and blue spots and blotches. When asked about the splotches, a woman with this name will most likely answer, "I fell down the stairs" or "But he loves me, he didn't mean it!"

Utopia (you-TOE-pee-uh) An imaginary place considered to be perfect. A name suitable for a metropolitan sex shop owner.

Valhalla (vaal-HAAL-uh) Where good Vikings go when they die. If you live in the Midwest, this name is to be avoided at all cost, lest too many Vikings fans try to find Odin's fabled hall.

Valva (VAL-vuh) A Korean knockoff of a famously safe Swedish automobile. Also, a lubricant used for race cars.

Vanilla (van-ILL-uh) Flavoring made from the vanilla bean. Boring or bland, e.g., "She didn't really look hot, she just looked Vanilla."

Vanity (VAN-ih-tee) Feelings of excessive pride. Vain, futile, or worthless. A child with this name will spend hours staring at herself in the mirror while you are forced to wait in the hall when you really, really have to go to the bathroom bad.

Velvet (VEHL-vet) A fabric with a dense pile. A girl with this name will most likely be a stripper. See also Cinnamon and Butterfly.

Victoria (vick-TOR-ee-uh) A girl with a really successful secret.

Vindalu (VIN-dahl-oo) A spicy Indian curry dish. The name will spur memories of bad meals and projectile diarrhea.

Virtue (VER-choo) Moral excellence and righteousness. Much like the male name Lucky, this moniker is bound to become an ironic joke for the child as those around her do their best to ensure that she, in fact, has no virtue. See also Chastity.

Vixen (VICKS-in) The female of a doglike species recognized by its pointy nose and ears, and renowned for its sneakiness. A malicious, fierce-tempered woman.

VulvaMae (vull-vah-MAY) The external genetalia of a female . . . Mae. The taunting will begin the moment the child enters kindergarten and will increase steadily before reaching a climax sometime around middle school and the introduction of sexual education. Popular nicknames for her will most likely be ClitorisMae and LabiaMae.

Waunice (wan-EECE) The light version of a Mexican beer made from black-eyed peas.

Westie (wehstee) Shortened name for the West Highland white terrior. A short-legged, mustached, long-coated female, generally of ill temper. A biter.

Whimsy (WHIM-zee) A quaint or fanciful quality. Female children given this name will have absolutely no ability to make rational decisions and most likely will devote their existence to hunting for faerie-folk in the wilderness.

Whisper (WHIS-purr) To utter very softly. This child will have a knack for walking through a room completely unnoticed. Professions to be considered should include ninja and cat burglar.

Wilma (WILL-muh) Wife of caveman. A child with this name will most likely marry a loud, verbally abusive braggart with a prominent forehead who can only afford to buy her one outfit and will make her propel the family automobile with her bare feet.

Winnagene (WIN-uh-jeen) A genetic lottery. Let's hope she's a big winner to help her overcome this terrible name.

Winnter (WHIN-tur) The coldest season of the year often characterized by coldness, misery, barrenness, or death. A child with this name will, no doubt, be described as frigid later in life.

Wirt (veert) A diminutive lump or protuberance found on the hands, feet, or genitalia. People will be reluctant to touch a girl with this name, afraid of catching her unattractiveness.

Xolani (zo-LAH-nee) African for "please forgive," which is undoubtedly what you'll be asking your child to do for you after a lifetime of having to spell this name for people ad nauseum.

Yadid (yeah-DID) The routine response to every mother's question beginning, "Have you . . . ?"

Yen (yehn) Japanese unit of currency. A female child with this name will, no doubt, take ironic joy every time some wisenheimer asks her how many of *her* it would take to buy a candy bar.

Yo (yoe) A casual greeting. This name becomes extremely troublesome when paired with the greeting itself, e.g., "Yo, Yo! How's it going?"

Young'n (YUNG-in) Hillbilly term meaning "small children," e.g., "I had four young'n until the twister done carried two of 'em off with the trailer house last summer."

Zelda (ZEL-duh) A telepathic princess kidnapped by the king of evil. A female child with this name will be driven insane by the endlessly looping and incredibly annoying theme music running through her head. Mommy and Daddy will most likely wake up one evening to see little Zelda standing over their bed with a kitchen knife preparing to slay the "minions of Ganon."

Zelpha (ZEL-fuh) A yellow staining gas with a foul egglike odor.

Zeruah (zehr-OO-wah) No meaning. But backward spells "HA! U R E Z" in vanity plate style.

Zestpoole (ZEHST-pool) A puddle of filth remarkable for its fresh, minty scent.